BECAUSE THERE IS JESUS

BECAUSE THERE IS JESUS

A Call to Be New-Made in Christ

**Homilies and Conferences
by Benedictine Archabbot
Lambert Reilly**

Abbey Press
St. Meinrad, IN 47577

© 1997 Saint Meinrad Archabbey
Published by One Caring Place
Abbey Press
St. Meinrad, IN 47577
1-800-325-2511
Call for complete catalog of publications.

Library of Congress Catalog Number
97-75019

ISBN 0-87029-305-2

Book design by Scott Wannemuehler

Printed in the United States of America

TABLE OF CONTENTS

Editor's Foreword

Anyone who has ever heard Archabbot Lambert Reilly, O.S.B., speak—and there are many thousands of you out there—knows that within this volume of his talks will be something very special: the words of a speaker whose style is downright riveting.

Even more riveting, however, is what Archabbot Lambert has to say when he's speaking. Readers of the present book will not have the benefit of his "live delivery," it is true. But the message he communicates here is, as ever, provocative, profound, prophetic...and no-nonsense. (I might add that readers will also find Archabbot Lambert's customary humor and wit not at all missing in these pages!)

But what is his no-nonsense *message*? It's in the book, on every page. As John Cardinal Newman (one of Archabbot Lambert's favorite spiritual guides), has said: *When a preacher dies and his sermons are collected, it's discovered he's preached only one theme.* In this volume we collect the sermons of a spiritual leader who all his life has preached only one theme: *Jesus.*

Because There Is Jesus. That is why the Gospel writers wrote the Gospels. That is why St. Benedict wrote the Holy Rule. That is why Archabbot Lambert Reilly, O.S.B., gave these talks and delivered them with such care and conviction.

When Jesus, the preacher, died, and his "sermons" were all collected in the Gospels, we found out that they were about only one thing, too: *love*—pure and simple.

Well, pure...but not simple. Archabbot Lambert Reilly's words help make it simpler, but not easy. May this, his "one-theme sermon"—*Because There Is Jesus*— help bring us all to one-theme living.

—*Linus Mundy, Publisher, Abbey Press*

To the monk,
heaven is next door.
He has no wish to see
farther in advance
of his journey than
where he is to make
his next step. He
plows and sows. He
prays, he meditates,
he studies, he writes,
he teaches, and then
he dies and goes
to heaven.
　　—Cardinal Newman

About the Homilies and Conferences

St. Benedict, in the Holy Rule, exhorts the abbot to meet regularly with his brethren. The abbot is to summon his brother monks to holiness and conversion, of course, but also to report on such daily importances as who is assigned to the baking of the bread, and who is receiving guests this week and who is to patch the roof. As the Abbot (from *abba*, meaning *father*), Lambert recognizes that *his* family is a very *human* family, like all of ours.

This is evidenced in a number of Archabbot Lambert's conferences with his community which are collected here. There is also a choice selection of his monastic preachings or homilies to folks beyond his community.

Says Archabbot Lambert in his first conference talk with his brother monks: "We're in a school, it's called the School of the Lord's Service, and I think it's extremely important that we have a steady flow of doctrine. Whether you believe it or not, I don't think I know everything. And so I will be asking other people to give conferences, also, but conferences we will have. There is a definition that goes: 'Education is moving forth from cocksure ignorance to thoughtful uncertainty.' I want to learn, and I want to learn from you, and I hope that you will learn from me. "

The presentations themselves took place between June, 1995, and July, 1997, all at St. Meinrad Archabbey. (Fr. Lambert was blessed as archabbot of his community in June of 1995.)

❧

Editor's Note: Much of Archabbot Lambert's spoken text in this book has been left unedited—the words are transcribed just as they were delivered.

It is intended that thus the reader will get a more true-to-life sense of the speaker's dynamic, "every-word-counts" preaching and teaching style.

BLESSED ARE THE MEEK

Coat of Arms
of The Right Reverend
Lambert Reilly, O.S.B.

The shield is divided into three sections by a chevron *sable* (black) charged with three roundels *argent* (silver) crossed sable. The chevron with its charges is taken from the Coat of Arms of St. Vincent Archabbey in Latrobe, Pennsylvania, where the bearer pursued advanced studies.

The field below the chevron *or* (gold) is charged with three crescent *gules* (red) from the Arms of the Seton family. Mother Seton is the foundress of the Mother Seton Sisters of Charity from whom the bearer received his early education and spiritual formation.

The field above the chevron *azure* (blue) is charged in chief dexter with a pierced star argent for the name Lambert which means "brightness" in honor of St. Lambert, bishop and martyr, the patron of the bearer, and in chief sinister azure is the hatchet argent, a symbol of martyrdom.

The motto "Blessed are the meek" refers to the heroic meekness of St. Lambert as depicted in the stained-glass window in the Archabbey Church at Saint Meinrad.

An Introduction
by Archabbot Lambert Reilly, O.S.B.

During 35 years of giving retreats, I have often been asked for copies of conferences and homilies. Having only sketchy notes, I have always been unable to say yes.

I never expected to publish. However, I never expected (or wanted) to give retreats either, but I did endlessly. So now, since I talk into a machine and Fr. Tobias transcribes, the possibility of passing on what I presently say and give to the monks is at hand.

Mother Teresa told me after a retreat I gave her and her sisters in Harlem: "Thank you, Father. So many retreat masters say: 'What can I tell you holy women?' You tell us to shape up and that's what we need to hear."

We Benedictines have a vow to "shape up." It's called "conversion of life." Not everybody has this challenge in vow form, but every follower of Jesus is told, "Learn of me." And that means endless conversion.

What I propose here is simple, direct and definitive. Each sentence requires digestion. I preach slowly and succinctly. This may be good to keep in mind since book form wasn't my concern in presenting these homilies and conferences.

My basic thought is: It doesn't matter if we do what we like. What matters is believing we're doing what God wills. That consoling truth has helped me throughout life and especially now, assuming the role as Abbot of our community when I feel like retiring.

This book is dedicated to my brother monks of
Saint Meinrad Archabbey,
who on rare occasions allow me to believe I'm a prophet
in my own home monastery.

Part I

Sermons from the Monastery

1.

YES, TO SUFFER

L et us get in on the conversation, and let's go with it far-ther than the Gospel account today takes us.

Peter says, "You are the Messiah." And Jesus responds, "The Heavenly Father told you this fact." And Jesus, again, "Now to continue and spell out this revelation, I'll tell you who the Messiah is; I'll define him. The Messiah is the one who has to suffer and die before rising. This further message I give you has the same strength of truth as my Father's ini-tial disclosure."

Peter accepts the Messiahship as such, but his own per-sonal definition of its meaning is not that of Christ. And he doesn't want Christ's definition to prevail. For him, the Messiah shouldn't suffer; for him, the Messiah shouldn't die. Far from it. And Jesus has to say, "My Messiahship will include suffering and death, and, not only mine, but yours, too. For every disciple will be a cross-bearer. There's no other possibility."

So Jesus says to Peter, "Get ready, because human logic—yours or anyone else's—isn't going to work. Figuring, planning, plotting, arranging on your part—none of these will have a chance in the life of a follower of mine."

Jesus says, "Peter, you are to provide the weakness; I'll bring the strength. The suffering will be there, and it will work." Jesus says, "Learn this, and relearn it all your life; and together we'll prevail. It will have to be acceptance on your part. Plans and dominance don't belong to you."

Jesus says, "Fear not your weakness. If you only give it to me, as your future cohort, Paul, will teach you, I'll work through your weakness. I'm master at such. It will always be that way, for you—and for everyone else."

And so it was for Peter, and so it was for Paul. Peter got himself thrown into prison; Jesus got him out. Paul knew every experience of difficulty; and Jesus afforded his own plan of release each time. So much for just a few facts in the lives of Peter and Paul.

Now, in claiming the feast for ourselves, the message is: It's our turn. We change the names—Peter and Paul—to our own names. The story's told about us. And that's all right, for that's the way it's supposed to be. Followers all know this experience, and as followers we need to put our "Amen" to the inevitable way of life a follower of Christ must know. Jesus said, "The Messiah must suffer and die, but in three days he will rise again." We must suffer and die, too. But we will also rise again. And the joy is that just as there was initial seating for Peter and Paul, so our place awaits us. Amen.

—June 29, 1995,
the Feast of Saints Peter and Paul.
Archabbey Church

2.

"How can This Be?"

Today we look at the scene from the view of Elizabeth. The child is leaping within her womb. She's filled with the Holy Spirit. Her husband is somewhere at hand, and the mother of her Lord visits. She says, "Blessed is she who believed what she was told." She knows what unbelief is like; she experiences it in her own home.

To bring all of this to its meaning, we go back to a particular day: Zachary, the priest, husband of Elizabeth, has been chosen by lot to go to the Altar of Incense. Each morning, each evening, there is a sacrifice offered in the Temple, and before the sacrifice in the morning and after the sacrifice in the evening there is incense. It's a magnificent day for Zachary.

He walks through the court of the Gentiles, the court of the women, the court of the men, into the sanctuary of the priests, and he goes beyond. And while he is there the Lord God speaks through his messenger, saying: "I have great plans. You and your wife will have a child. He'll be in those plans." Zachary and Elizabeth have prayed for years to no effect. They're still praying.

When Zachary is told that his prayer has been answered, he asks, "How can this be?" He's asking because he doubts. He's saying by his question, "I am an old man, my wife is an old woman: such don't have children." He's told, "Zachary, you have talked too much. Now be quiet." And Zachary will be quiet until he can write, "John is his name." Elizabeth knows about this. When he comes home, he can't talk. It's because he didn't believe.

And then there's that other scene. There's no walking

through a temple; there's just the privacy of a home. And there is a young woman and she is praying, and she is praying the way prayer truly is prayer: She's praising God. And of a sudden she has a visitor—it's the same that Zachary knew—and she's told, "God has a plan, and you will be special and he, your Son, will be the Savior."

And Mary asks the question with the same words, but it's not, "How can this be?" Rather, it's "How can this be that God works this way with me?" It's not to question as if God can't do; it's in complete wonderment.

Zachary learns in time—Mary knows from the beginning—God does what God does. Zachary comes with the fullness of his mind; and Mary comes with a heart open to whatever God wants. The Word of God says it so beautifully, "She ponders in her heart." Not with knowledge, but with acceptance.

St. Ambrose tells us that Mary's life is a rule of life for all of us. We're all so filled with the Zachary, we're all so filled with our knowledge, we're all so filled with our question that every time something happens we don't understand, "How can this be?!"

But Mary, she's the one; and she shows us the way. Mary is Our Lady of Einsiedeln. In the Carmelite monasteries today, she's Our Lady of Mount Carmel. We all have our particular approach with devotion.

Mary speaks directively once, and the same message comes in any apparition that is authentic: "Do whatever He tells you." He talks to us all the time in the circumstances of our life, and we beg Mary of Einsiedeln today that we may be like her, that we may ask by way of exclamation, "How can this be!"

If we do, then Mary is truly with us, and where Mary is, there is Jesus. Because as Pope Paul VI tells us, we go to Mary for only one reason: to find Jesus in her arms. This, I hazard, is how Elizabeth saw it. This, I hope, is how we may see it from hereon, today. Amen.

—July 16, 1995,
The Feast of Our Lady of Einsiedeln.
Archabbey Church

3.

BEING TRULY KIND

M y brothers and sisters, and especially my brothers and sisters who are co-workers...

The Gospel account today is one that disturbs a number of people. They think of Martha as being treated unfairly. She's doing the work; Mary's doing nothing. And Mary gets the praise. I think it's safe to say the Lord God—and Jesus is the Lord God—doesn't make any mistakes, doesn't say the wrong things. We'd better take a new look at the reading if this is our thought.

Jesus is on his way to Jerusalem; he's on his way to suffer and die. He knows this; it's a matter of time. On his way to Jerusalem, he decides to stop at the home of friends. Evidently, he's been at their home many times. Evidently, he has had many good meals at their home. But when he comes today, it's a little different; he's heavy, he's burdened. He's like us in all things, save sin. Knowing what is to come, he's weary.

Martha sees him coming, and Martha moves according to her regular approach: Since he's here, I'm going to give him a meal. And so, after a greeting, Martha goes off on her own. Mary, on the other hand, sits down with Jesus. She wants to see what he is like today. Martha, in the kitchen building up the meal, is getting a little excited. "I'm doing everything, she's doing nothing," and the thoughts finally form words, and she says to Jesus, "Why don't you send her in here?"

Evidently, Mary helped at other times. Jesus says, "Martha, you're busy about many things, but Mary has taken the better approach. Leave her alone!" Jesus is saying in effect to Martha, "Today isn't a day when I want much eating; I'm not up to it. If I wanted anything, perhaps the most would be a sandwich."

Martha has decided what Jesus needs; and he's going to get it! Mary sits down and finds out what's in him, and what he wants. What we have in Martha is a case of "unkind kindness." This is a case of what we might call "misplaced kindness." We all know what it's like, how people sometimes don't treat us as we know we should be treated or want to be treated. Let me tell you several little stories and maybe the point will come clear.

The first time I was in San Diego to give a retreat, I finished the retreat—and when I finish a retreat I'm dead, because during the retreat I get all wound up and excited and, you know, this goes on for days. And when the retreat is over, all I want to do is sit, collapse—I hazard the statement— say nothing. But I do want to be just sort of at rest.

Well, I finished this retreat and I discovered I had about six hours before the plane was to leave. I knew some people who had moved to San Diego, and I thought, "I'll try to contact them." I contacted them; everything was going to be wonderful. I was gonna go to their home and sit and rest. They lived close to where I was, not too far from the airport, and since they were free that day, they would be glad to come and get me.

So, waiting, wanting to get away, desiring a few moments of quiet, I got there. I no sooner got there than one member of the family said, "This is your first time in San Diego?" and I said, "Yes." "That means, then, you haven't seen the San Diego Zoo." "No, I haven't." "Well, the San Diego Zoo is the best zoo in the world so you must see it." It wasn't long we were at the San Diego Zoo. The monkeys were looking at us, we were looking at them, and I thought they had a better view.

So often we know just what the other person needs, and God pity him or her if that person is not ready for all the kindness we can heap upon them!

The second little story: I was out for dinner. Somebody else was treating. You know what happens when that happens: one eats and eats and eats. The meal was delicious. But when it was time to leave, somebody in the crowd said, "Why don't we stop at so-and-so's house?" Well, being polite like Dear Abby suggests, we called the home. "Oh yes, they were free; they'd be thrilled if we could come." We got to the home and the first thing we heard was, "I have just baked a German chocolate cake." "Thank you. No, thank you." "I would be extremely insulted if you wouldn't have it." And so we all had German chocolate cake, and I can speak only for myself, but the rest of the night it was Pep-to Bis-mol!

There's a very important lesson in this Gospel. The Lord wasn't saying that Martha did anything bad. The Lord said Mary had chosen the better part. Evidently Martha had chosen the good part. And since all of us in the following of Christ are invited to become always better people, perhaps there's really a message here: There is a certain thing about charity where it can be forced and where it can be exquisite, because it learns. And so I say to all of us: Perhaps we ought to forget the stories that would equal the ones I told, and instead of looking to how people have not treated us as we would have liked, let's move to look at how we treat others. Let's look to how we can be truly kind.

Ignatius of Antioch was on the way to Rome to become a martyr; it's the only thing he wanted. It's hard to believe, but it was. And he wrote to the Romans and he said, "Don't do anything to hold me back. If you would, it would be misplaced kindness."

We're all different, all of us. We have different likes and different dislikes. It's good for all of us to learn from each other what pleases. And then, if we can help bring this about, let's move toward it. This is truly, truly Christian. Amen.

—July 23, 1995.
Archabbey Church

4.

Two Guys in School

O ur Holy Father St. Benedict tells us that the Gospel is our guide. On this occasion of jubilee, we look to the Gospel to be guided. This means, then, today we can look at knocking, and we can look at seeking.

Regarding knocking, the Gospel story encourages the owner to get up and give the intruder what he wants, thereby fending off his persistence. The Rule of Benedict demands that the monks not open the gate; rather, let the inquirer persist for days in his request. In the Gospel, what's wanted by the one knocking are supplies to be carried off. In the Rule, what's wanted by the one knocking is entrance and life to be lived within.

In reference to seeking, in the Gospel, what's sought is clearly bread—bread for a visiting friend to make a meal. In the Rule, what's sought is permanent residence, to make a life. The Gospel account makes it clear that the Lord always gives good gifts, gifts better than any human answering any request can. And this is because the knocking and the seeking goes to the Lord God, the Lord God who is called, "Our Father, who art in heaven."

When we go now from the Gospel and the Rule, we look specifically to two monks who 50 years ago knocked, and to two monks who 50 years later still seek. When they started knocking at our monastery gate, they were 10 in number. Fifty years ago on their profession day, besides Hilary and Prosper there were Xavier, Blaise, George, Odo, Virgil, Odilo, Fidelis and Marcian. Several of these 10 have died. Several have gone on to another way of life. And several celebrate this year at Blue Cloud Abbey, our daughter house located in the state of South Dakota.

But our brothers Hilary and Prosper are still with us here. They're the reason for gathering today in celebration. Once accepted into the monastery, their seeking of God, ongoing as it was and is, has shown itself in very different ways.

Father Hilary comes from a little town in Indiana called St. Thomas. It's near the big city of Vincennes. Father Hilary, after profession and ordination, went off to school, and he got a doctorate, a doctorate in French. Some people tell me he speaks French flawlessly, as if he were born to the language. Father Hilary taught for a number of years; he was Rector of the seminary for a number of years, and then he moved on. He's been in Beech Grove—that's near the big city of Indianapolis—and Father Hilary has been engaged now for a number of years in ministry to priests. He's been chaplain to the Benedictine Sisters, and he has traveled the world. It was nice that his schedule allowed him to be here today.

Father Prosper comes from a little town in Indiana called St. Henry; St. Henry is near the big town of Ferdinand. Father Prosper, after profession and ordination, went off to school, and for a number of years taught Greek. They tell me Father Prosper knows the New Testament very well in the original language. Father Prosper went on to become bi-ritual, meaning that he offers the Eucharist not only in the Roman rite but also in the Byzantine. Father Prosper then didn't go to the big city; he went to the hermitage. He went to the beef farm, and there he has lived in prayer. Father Prosper travels the world, not the way Father Hilary does, but by prayer. And our community has been blessed that God has called one of us to such a life. They tell me—and they don't have to tell me, I know—that Father Prosper is a gourmet cook, and there is an orange liqueur that he can make from orange skins like unto which no one else has recipe for.

The lives of Father Hilary and Father Prosper have differed one from another, just as their lives have differed from ours. It's good for us to remind ourselves that there is no one way for the seeking of God to unfold, even though the early knocking is that which we all experience in common.

We all have our ideas of how monks should live; we have our ideas of what confreres should do. But there is a Lord God who somehow says, "I am the Lord God and I do whatever I will." And that Lord God gets us where he wants us.

The monastery is a School of the Lord's Service, and no one graduates from it. Each one's life in that monastic living is unique in its seeking. After 50 years, we still encourage our confreres to truly, truly seek God. For this is the only reason there is a gate to knock at. Seeking God is the means whereby God is found. And God is found here, and then he's found forever in the eternal life to which we're all called. As Teresa of Avila says so simply and beautifully, "We don't build our lives on a bridge." And that's all we're on presently.

Father Hilary, Father Prosper, continue to teach us in your own way what seeking God means. And then, some day, when we don't talk about death, we'll all be together forever and ever. Amen.

—July 30, 1995,
on the Fiftieth Jubilee of Profession of
Fr. Hilary Ottensmeyer, O.S.B.,
and Prosper Lindauer, O.S.B.
Archabbey Church

5.

MERCY

It was at least 20 years ago, and we were very high up. I was in the State of Ancash, in the country of Peru, in South America. We had a priory there. On Thursday morning the Prior, Fr. Joel, said to me, "Let's go to the marketplace." There were only about two villages that were higher up than where the priory was located.

When we got to the marketplace, the people from those higher territories came to barter, to trade. I found myself from the beginning the center of attention. People were pointing at me and I couldn't understand why. Fr. Joel explained to me, from what he heard them say—because I'm a "gringo"—that they'd never seen gray hair before. They came closer. There was more pointing. I found out they had never seen blue eyes before. The group surrounded me and followed me.

We were trying to make some exchange, because you just don't buy and sell, and Fr. Joel said we had come to a good deal. Now watch me. I took my fingers like this [joining thumb and forefinger in a circle] to indicate I wanted the deal, and I said, "Good." In that part of the world, I found out, that when the fingers are like this it indicates the person is a homosexual. Fr. Joel said, "Let us get you out of here immediately."

Being "ugly Americans," we can say, "They've never seen gray hair or blue eyes! And they have that stupid symbol!" But let the story stand.

About 10 years ago I was in a town called Pocahontas. It's in the state of Arkansas and that's in the United States. There was a meeting going on, and I was asked to attend the meeting by the bishop. There was discussion on the bishops writing a pastoral letter on women.

When I got there, there were about 50 lay women, probably about 35 religious sisters, and in the distance I saw one other male figure. There was a sister who was in charge of it all. She had a control group with her. She was explaining what the day would be like. She started by saying that we'll give numbers—1, 2, 3, 4, 5, 6—and we'll do this all around. And then all the 1's will go together, and the 2's will go together, and we'll have small group discussion. She said that when the small group assembles, each group will choose a secretary—a person who will write things down and report back later to the big group—and will also choose a facilitator, the one who will read the questions and keep everything going.

So we knew what we were going to do. And then the numbers were given out, but that other male figure on the other side of the room and I didn't get any numbers. I thought I'd walk over and say hello to him. As I was on my way, there was a group that had already gathered together, and a particular sister in the group said, "I don't think it's right, Father. Everybody was invited. You people should get numbers as well as the rest of us." A lay woman in the group said, "I think it's right. It's about time these men are treated the way we're treated all the time." I didn't say anything. (I was amazed at myself!)

I went over to meet the other male figure, discovering— and this is an aside—that his name was Lambert. He said to me, "A woman from the control group came over and said, 'When you two meet, don't let the priest be the secretary. We're sick and tired of hearing priests talk.'" I didn't say anything.

As we began, the sister who was in charge of the control group, not knowing what one from the group had already said, came over and said, "Now you two are going to have to figure out who will be facilitator and who will be secretary." And I said, "Oh, that's already decided." And she said, "Who do you think you are to have made that decision?" I didn't say anything, but I want to tell you what I could have said. I could have said, "I have spent 30 years of my life giving retreats to sisters, and there's no sister I have ever dealt with who has thrown remarks at me like you have." I didn't say that; I didn't say anything. I was so surprised at myself.

Pocahontas is a high place in Arkansas. I want to go to a third high place, where we get some kind of directive. The high place is the Mount of the Beatitudes. There is a particular Beatitude that we all need to dwell on in connection with what's been said today. The Beatitude says: "Blessed are the merciful."

There are all kinds of definitions of mercy. We're told that mercy is the best translation for *hesed* from the Hebrew. We're told by St. Thomas Aquinas that mercy is love shown to the absolutely unworthy. We're told by Pope John Paul II that mercy is love's best face. We're told that mercy is love pushed to the wall. We're told you can't go beyond mercy in love because it's the end of the line.

What does mercy tell us? Mercy tells us we're all different. Mercy tells us cultures are different. Mercy tells us peoples are different. And mercy says, "That's all right!" Mercy also teaches us tolerance and forgiveness. Generally, we're not tolerant of other people's views because we can't understand that they have backgrounds and experiences and temperaments and thought patterns that are different from ours. Somehow everybody has to be the same as we are, and then when they act the way they do we project the guilt that would be ours if we were the ones acting it out.

If we could realize that each one is an individual gift of God, and that each one has a background, an education, a temperament, a make-up, a home that is different from everyone else's, then somehow we might be able to tolerate views that don't fit with ours.

Mercy is not agreement; mercy is not saying everything's all right. But mercy somehow says, "We're different. We should be kind, no matter what, and in time, with love from both sides, things will work out."

17

The reason we have this challenge is that the mercy of God endures forever. The reason we have this challenge is everyone of us wants mercy. The reason we have this challenge is it's mercy that helps people become saints.

In all the other Beatitudes there's something in the beginning and something different in the end. "Blessed are the poor in spirit, the kingdom of heaven is theirs." But with this particular Beatitude there's the same thing in the beginning and the end: "Blessed are the merciful, for they shall obtain mercy."

If we're not understood and we're not accepted and we're not tolerated and we're not forgiven, it easily may be because we don't do it. We want it; but we don't do it. It's so strange that we all have the almighty mind that indicates that whatever we think is exactly correct. The truth of the matter is we're all called to have the almighty mind which is in Christ Jesus. And acceptance and tolerance and forgiveness are his watchwords.

Everyone of us can say over and over again what we hear so directly from another Gospel, which was preached on so eloquently here in this church not many days ago, "Lord, be merciful to me, a sinner."

My novice master used to say there's only one success that God acknowledges, and that's sanctity. And to become a saint means to become more and more and more merciful. This message is for me; this message is for you; it's for all of us. It would be marvelous if today this feast brought this home a little more clearly, because we hear over and over again in the liturgy that we are to live out Him whom we have received. We are somehow to act out the Word which has come within.

You want to be understood. I do, in the job I have. And if you want to be understood, and you want to be accepted— and I do, too—then show mercy, and mercy will be yours. And let me show mercy, and mercy will be mine. It's a great day. It's a marvelous day. It's a wonderful feast, and we've been to the hills, and we're on "The Holy Hill" here.

Wouldn't it be wonderful if it could be said because it would be true: "At Saint Meinrad, Indiana, there's mercy every-where. It's overflowing." Pray God. Pray God. Amen.

—November 1, 1995,
on the Feast of All Saints.
Archabbey Church

6.

GOING HIS WAY

My brothers...

It is said that a preacher is most effective when he preaches first to himself. Thinking that he is normal enough, then what he has to say out loud can go to others who are like he is. Tonight, if I use the word "you," it's I first of all speaking to myself. And I hope that the message that I need to hear may be one that will benefit you, too.

When things don't go as we want them to, we're angry. When people say what we don't want them to say, we're angry. When the community makes a decision contrary to ours, we're angry. When the Church issues a decree that we disagree with, we're angry. There are big things we're angry at. There are little things we're angry at. We have a built-in facility for thinking that we know. And we have a built-in facility for wanting all things to flow according to that knowledge.

Tonight I ask the question: Who do you [pointing first to himself and then to all], who do you think you are, that things should go the way you think they should? Big things or small things. Who do you think you are, that people should act the way you want them to? Who do you think you are, that plans are only good if you are somehow the master craftsman for them?

After asking this question—and you can continue it for yourself, as I can for myself—we move to the question: Is there anyone who has a right to have things go his or her way? Is there anyone who is always right in his thinking? Is

21

there anyone who should be able to call every shot that is called? Well, there is someone. It isn't you; it isn't I. It's the Lord God. He alone has the right, and he alone, by the way, is the one who is always right.

But when he gave us free will—and he gave every one of us free will—he gave the right to have things go his way away. He gave us the right to say yes or no to him. He gave us the right to run to him or run far from him. He gave us the right to be in alignment or to be in disobedience. And if he is the only one who has the right to have his mind always—the mind that should be followed—and he has given that right away, then who do we think we are?

And how does he treat us who don't agree with him, starting with me, and moving to every one of you? How does he treat you when you go your way and not his? How does he treat you when you insist on having the almighty mind when he is the Almighty? He treats you with tolerance and forgiveness. And he gives you this as gift. You, starting with me, you don't deserve this; he gives it to you freely. And every gift that he gives, we are to give to each other.

The Lord has brought us together. We come from different backgrounds. We come from different minds. We come with different educations. We're not all artists, or architects...or geniuses. But he has brought us together, and we will find salvation that will lead us to him if we treat one another as he treats each and every one of us. And that is with tolerance and forgiveness.

Anger, when it stays within us, destroys us and destroys the community. Anger that stays within us is that which leads to the vice that St. Benedict says must be rooted out—the vice he calls murmuring. The anger either turns to an internal murmuring—which we think doesn't show itself, and, oh my, does it!—or it turns itself to an external murmuring whereby certain people are the ones we talk to, certain people are the ones we associate with, certain people who have sense enough and culture enough to be like we are and be our companions. And the rest can go their merry way.

Anger is so destructive. If it destroys me, it destroys you. If it destroys you, it destroys me. And that anger will stay, and it will show itself, even though we're clever and try to cover it, unless we learn to tolerate and to forgive.

Whom are the people we live with? Weak sinners striving in this School to follow the Lord. And who are we, who am I, who live with them? We are exactly the same. I'm exactly the same. We can sing the most beautiful hymns, we can have the best liturgies, we can have the best books read, but if we are unwilling to tolerate and forgive each other over and over and over again, endlessly, then we're here, but we're not in the School of the Lord's Service learning.

Tonight, in case you're not sure of the reflection, tonight I suggest that you—starting with me, and going to every one of you—I suggest that you look to your heart, and to root out the anger by asking for forgiveness, and by remembering that we will be forgiven as we forgive, and by remembering that forgiveness is the gift which, freely given, must freely be shared. Amen.

—December 19, 1995,
Advent Reconciliation Service.
Archabbey Church

7.

MAKING ROOM

When Christmas comes each year, there are certain people we inevitably think of. Tonight I'm thinking of a woman who was a big woman—big bodily, big in every sense. She was a woman who was thought by some to be incapable of being in charge, and yet she was in charge of almost everything. When she died—and I had the honor of preaching her funeral homily—I remember saying she was a woman who could rule a city from a desk.

She spent her entire religious life with people who used to be spoken of as retarded. She knew all the language—"trainable," "educable"—but she knew before others did that the ones she dealt with were exceptional. She started out in a home that could hardly be called that. She dealt with architects as time went on—among them, the famous Belli & Belli of St. Louis—and she built a home in Greensburg, Pennsylvania, that became a model.

There was something that happened at that home one Christmas, and that's why I especially think of her tonight. The children with learning disabilities were presenting a Christmas play for their parents. The production had three acts. The opening scene was at Nazareth, featuring the decree of Caesar Augustus. The second scene was in Bethlehem, featuring the refusal of the innkeeper. The third act was to be the manger site in the hill country.

The faculty, the parents, and this marvelous woman, Sister Celine, were anxious about the children's ability to perform properly. To their delight, the first act came off very well. In the second act, all was going well, too. Joseph and Mary knocked on the door of the inn, and were politely and quickly refused entrance by the little innkeeper, Danny. He spoke his words forcefully and clearly: "There is no room." He was the one who had to be coaxed along. He wasn't able to do much at all. He was told, "When you hear the knock, say your few words, 'There is no room.'"

The first time he said it. The second time he heard the knock, Mary and Joseph pleaded again, and this time very sorrowfully. Danny hesitated a bit, but then again he said his line, "There is no room." The script called for one more knock, one more plea, one more refusal. This time Joseph begged for a room with all his heart. The little innkeeper boldly began his refusal, but could not continue. Instead, he simply broke down, sobbing and saying, "You can have my room."

The teachers struggled courageously to get the play back on track. But it didn't work. But the audience saw demonstrated in the boy the true meaning of Christmas.

Tonight, because of Sister Celine and Danny, I want to remind us that, to some degree, all of us play the role of the innkeeper; we accept or we reject others. Are we more like the original innkeeper who turned the Holy Family out into the lonely, cold night? Or are we like the small child who welcomed them in?

It may be that we hang "No Vacancy" signs around us frequently, by rude words or gestures or tone of voice, telling others clearly, "We don't want to be bothered. We're too busy. We're too tired." And if we are in an exclusive mood, catering only to the better class of people, chances are we would have turned away Joseph and Mary, too. And in doing that we would have rejected Jesus himself, hidden under his mother's heart.

Some people are strictly unbending in excluding, while others believe that there's always room for one more. Of Mother Teresa of Calcutta, who has helped more than a million people die with a bit of dignity, it's said that she always makes room for one more, no matter who.

Tonight I wonder: I wonder what Jesus was thinking of

in later life when he said, "Whatsoever you do for others, you do for me." Could he not have been reflecting back to the very day of his birth and the rejection seen at the Bethlehem Inn?

We all know Christmas is the traditional season of giving. But the better gifts are not the material ones. A true and beautiful present for another is a bit of our time, when we know there's none to spare. A little advice and direction, if we are so blessed and can give it, when another is in need, is another beautiful gift. We can give a simple, silent smile of friendliness to one hurting, whose life may be filled with confusion and pain.

This feast tells us Jesus left a secure home in heaven and came to earth as a little child and grew up just like the little innkeeper in the Christmas play. Jesus invites us to his house, not for one night's shelter, but forever, where there's a mansion especially prepared for each one of us.

And our means of being welcome and attaining such can be learned from the slow-learning child, Danny, who made room for Jesus. Anytime we make room for anyone, it's Jesus we welcome. Isn't this the message of Christmas? In our lives shouldn't we rewrite the script, "There was no place for them in the inn"? I think so. Sister Celine, God rest her, thought so. And Danny, if he still be with us, knows so. Amen.

—*December 25, 1995, Christmas*
Midnight Mass.
Archabbey Church

8.

GOD SPEAKS

My brothers and sisters...

St. Therese of Lisieux wrote: "If I had no faith, I would
have inflicted death on myself without a moment's hesita-
tion." Without faith it's impossible to please God. To live
without pleasing God is impossible; there is no life without it.

We hasten to God, as Augustine tells us, not by running,
but by believing. Faith is all-important. We ask the question—
which every seeker asks: Whom are we to believe, so we can
know what to believe?

St. Thomas Aquinas says we believe for two reasons:
what's told us is possible, and the teller is reliable. With God,
all things are possible. And God can neither deceive nor be
deceived; so God is the one to be believed. If we're sure that
God speaks, and we know what he says, things can be fine.

Well, God speaks. God the Father speaks; God the Son
speaks; God the Holy Spirit speaks. And each says the same
thing. Sometimes it seems that God's message is too simple,
and, at the same time, too difficult. But Benedict of Nursia
didn't think so. He heard the Father; he heard the Son; he
heard the Holy Spirit. What was said was simple; but what
was said was accepted as difficult.

The Heavenly Father breaks the silence of heaven three
times—turn the pages of the New Testament and find it out.
Twice, when the Heavenly Father speaks, he makes the message so clear. The first time he speaks is at the baptism of
Jesus: "This is my beloved Son." At the Transfiguration, when
every sign is there that the Son is the fulfillment of the

Prophets and the Law, when every power is seen to radiate from him, through the face that's shining like the sun, and the garments like the snow, the Heavenly Father repeats, and adds: "The is my beloved Son; pay attention to him." That's the message of the Heavenly Father. It's simple; it's difficult.

The Second Person of the Blessed Trinity is that Son, and he speaks in total agreement with the Father. He says: "Learn of me. I am the Way. No one goes to the Father except through me." He praises other people: John the Baptist is the greatest born of woman. He praises his Blessed Mother: No one ever heard the Word of God and kept it better. But He doesn't say: "Be like them"; he says: "Be like I am." Mary is the greatest and the first Christian because no one ever heard that Word and kept it better. Her life is a total reflection of Christ's.

And then there is the Holy Spirit, and he is God. And Jesus says, the "Holy Spirit will come to bring to mind everything that I have taught." And the only thing that Christ ever taught was Himself. And so the Holy Spirit is with the Church until the end of time, to enable us in every age to say, "Jesus Christ is Lord." Cardinal Newman says so simply: "The Holy Spirit doesn't come to replace Jesus. He comes that Jesus may come in his coming." Jesus. Jesus; all Benedict does is point out Jesus. Nineteen times explicitly, and in the Rule that is so short, he says in one way or another, "Prefer no one and nothing to Christ." And every word on every other page of that "little Rule for beginners" says the same thing implicitly.

He establishes a School of the Lord's Service for that one purpose: to focus, to live, to become Christ. In that school, no one graduates. In that school, the lesson is always the same. In that school, there is striving to come away from the excuses that hold back the call of Christ. "I have a mother. I have a father." So what? "I have someone to bury." There will always be someone to bury. The Rule says over and over again, "Come away, come to," and it says so forcefully in so many different ways, "Come away from self."

The follower of Christ can't be too tired to pray. The follower of Christ can't be someone who is inconvenienced by the demands of the life. The follower of Christ has to be involved in the totality of Christ-seeking.

When we come to the monastery, we have someone who is our teacher. *Unus est magister.* There is one teacher, and that teacher when we come is the novice master. And my novice master would say repeatedly, "There is only one success that God acknowledges and that is Christ-likeness."

St. Benedict, we're told, couldn't have lived other than he taught. So he lived Christ, and the process moved in development of living Christ more fully. And then he died. And he had to hear the words of the heavenly Father, "Come in. You've learned the lesson. I see my Son in you." We come to the monastery to live well so that we die well. And in the monastery it's Christ; it's Christ. Forget "me," whoever the "me" is. St. Benedict spells this lesson out in a way that's uniquely Benedictine. But there is no other message to be spelled out, no matter what one's vocation.

Last night some of us gathered around the beds of two of our brethren who are close to death. And with the intercession of Our Holy Father, and the imminence of the feast, we anointed them: Fr. Dunstan and Br. Rene. And our prayer is, as is the prayer of the Church in the ceremony, that the movement into Christ may develop, and then life takes on more meaning.

My brothers and sisters, it isn't hard to know what God wants; it's difficult to do what God wants. And that's why we can say with the word of God—and it says it in many different ways—"Put on the mind which is in Christ Jesus." Pope John Paul II says, in such a simple way, "Jesus is the only answer." Whatever the problem, we have to figure it out in him. And we have to move toward self-giving, and not hold on to the mind that is our own, that holds us back.

This is a glorious feast. It gives meaning to all of this. As we look at that [stained glass] window down there, Benedict ascends. He's at home. We're not; we're just on our way. And he shows us the way to go, and the Way is Jesus Christ.

One little prayer: Holy Father Benedict, pray for us, that we may be worthy of the promises of Christ. Amen.

—March 21, 1996,
the Feast of St. Benedict.
Archabbey Church

9.

ALLELUIA

My brothers and sisters…

The Easter message haunts human logic. If one starts with the thought that people don't rise from the dead, a foresworn conclusion has already been realized. If one starts with the realization that God's ways aren't ours, then one can come to a very different judgment regarding the eternal Galilean.

This feast of feasts isn't a question for logic. It's a matter of, and for, the deepest faith possible. Christ died around 3:00 in the afternoon. Joseph of Arimathea had to get to Pilate quickly, because at 6:00 in the evening the Sabbath started, and ended work—even the process of burial.

Was everything as it should be at the tomb, Joseph of Arimathea's tomb, now to be the tomb of Jesus? For answer, enter the women, caregivers supreme, even in death. They will find out how things are. They find, and they find out more than they bargained for. Thinking they were going to a dead body, they experience an earthquake, an angel, an angel's message, and its fulfillment in the no-longer-dead person of the alive and risen, death-conquering Jesus, who tells them there's no longer reason—ever—for fear.

It's at that moment that their faith passes over to knowledge, afforded by sight and hearing and touch. And their knowledge now allows for the surety of our faith. They find out—and we must find out, it's our turn now—that Jesus is not a figure in a book; he's a living presence. It may be we start out studying about Jesus, but we, because of this Easter

Day, end up meeting him in flesh that dies no more.

They find out—and we must find out, it's our turn now—that Jesus is not a memory. As the Greeks tell us, the dearest memory fades, and time wipes out all things. But not Jesus. He can't be of the past, because he is life. And life is present, ever present, never, ever dying again.

They find out—and we must find out, it's our turn now—that there's an endless depth in Christian faith; it never stands still. It enables us to know him better and better. What more can we ask for? The answer is: nothing.

We have looked forward to Holy Easter with joy and spiritual longing, as Our Holy Father Benedict invited us at the outset of Lent. And now—and now—that joy is ours. If we fear less now than before, Easter has truly taken hold of us. And its "alleluias" are ours.

We have nothing to fear... because Christ has died, Christ is risen, Christ will come again. And so our alleluias are without end. Amen.

—Easter Sunday,
April 7, 1996.
Archabbey Church

10.

No-Nonsense People

I think we can safely say there are three, for sure, no-nonsense people. These three are Jesus, Mary, and John the Baptist. They're no-nonsense people because what they think doesn't get clouded and overtaken by their own thought pattern. Their thought pattern is totally identified with the truth. Jesus says, "Learn of me. I am the truth." Mary says, "Do whatever he tells you." And John the Baptist says, "He must increase, I must decrease."

These three no-nonsense people have background for their approach. Jesus is the God-Man. When he is born, the Word becomes flesh. There's no taint of sin, no need for mix-up. When Mary is born, she's born having been conceived without sin. There's no taint of sin in her; there's no mix-up. John the Baptist is believed to have been born without sin because, so to speak, he was baptized in the womb when Jesus first met him, and the first meeting with Jesus is baptism. And so they're different from the rest of us.

We, born with sin, have a darkened intellect. And the greatest prerogative of the darkened intellect is to think that it is always right. That's why then, because our intellect is darkened, we all have a common call, and that is to give up our thinking and take on the thinking of Christ.

The birth of Jesus was certainly special. We have read about the birth of John the Baptist. And it seems that no interviewers got to Ann and Joachim for details of the birth of Mary.

John the Baptist has a lot to say, but he says it so simply—and truth is always connected with simplicity. He says

to everybody, "Go to him," implying "Become like him." And
he spells out what "going to him" means. And what does this
Christ say? He says to people in general, "If you have two
coats, and somebody doesn't have any, well, give one away."
That's the kind of mind he has. That's what you have to take
on. "If you have enough for two to eat, and one doesn't have
something to eat, supply that one. Give up your thinking of
holding and hoarding, because that's a product of the fallen
intellect, and take on the thinking that is mine, that is really
the true Way."

Then, when John the Baptist talks to individual people
with his simplicity, he gives the same message. He says to the
soldier, "Do what you're supposed to do, and don't bully."
He says to the tax collector, "Collect what you're supposed to
collect, and don't cheat."

John's idea always is bringing the individual into the
fullness of truth, which means growth in Christ. The beauty
of this is, as the document *On the Church in the Modern World*
tells us, the more we become like Christ, the more truly
human we become.

Now, a year ago I was blessed as the abbot of this
monastery, and my desire should be to be a no-nonsense person, and to say things very directly and simply. This, then,
means I should say, speaking generally, "Do what is good,
avoid what is evil, let the judgment of that goodness be the
standard of Christ." Then I should say to monks, "If you're
monks, then live the life of monks. If you're monks, then live
the life you have pledged. If you're monks, then live according to the custom of your monastery. Get up in the morning.
Go to choir. Be where you're supposed to be. Don't follow
what your own fallen intellect thinks, which equates itself
with truth according to your judgment. But remember: You
have decided to walk according to someone else's judgment.
Remember: There is no one whom you're going to prefer to
Christ."

Now, when one takes this approach, the approach of
John the Baptist, he has to remember there's the possibility he

36

may lose his head. Remember: Herod said, "Give me the head of John on a plate." When John got to Herod, he got very specific. He said, "The one you call your wife isn't; she belongs to a relative. Get rid of her."

John teaches us—and it's not only John, but it's Jesus and Mary, too—that if you're going to be a witness, you have to be willing to be a martyr. And if you're not willing to be a martyr, then keep quiet. You know, it's so easy to champion a cause until one has to pay for the cause one champions.

And so I would say that what I wish for myself today— to move into the spirit of John the Baptist—is the wish that I would wish for all of you. Because this is what the world needs, the big world, and the little world in which we live. It needs people who do what they say they will do. It needs people who live what they have pledged themselves to live. And the reward? It brings them into the personality of Christ, it brings them into the fullness of humanity, and it brings them the promise that where Jesus is, and Mary is, and John is, that's where we will be.

It's a great feast. It's a nice one to celebrate in connection with the blessing of an abbot. I hope its message comes clear, first of all to the preacher, and to those who have been willing to listen. Amen.

—June 24, 1996,
Feast of St. John the Baptist.
Renovation Chapel

11.

ON THE WAY

It's Caesaria Philippi, and Jesus asks the question, "Well, who do people think I am?" Their answers are good ones: "He's somebody special. He's somebody special from God." And then the next question: "If that's what people think, and you're the people close to me, what do you think?" And then Peter answers, for those close to him, "You are the Messiah, the Son of the living God." And Jesus says, "Peter, you couldn't know it on your own. It's a revelation. My Father has spoken to you."

Now we move on. Jesus says, "I'm the Messiah, the Son of the living God, and I'm going to tell you what the Messiah is here for. I'm going to define 'Messiah.' The Messiah is the Suffering Servant. I'm going to go and I'm going to give all." And Peter, who had been blessed by the heavenly Father with the correct answer, is now invaded by the devil. And Peter says, in effect, "I don't accept that definition. You can't do that. No. No way." And Jesus says, "Let me identify you. You're aligned with Satan. Get behind me."

And then Jesus goes on to say—catch this—"If I am the Messiah, and the Messiah is the Suffering Servant, and you are my disciples, then you'll share in being the Suffering Servant. And let me tell you how much you'll share in that. If you are my disciple, you'll take up your cross daily, and you'll come after me."

Jesus is loud; he's clear; he's exact; he's direct. "You'll have to make up in your bodies what I allow to be lacking in mine. The identification has to be so close that where I am, you are."

Peter didn't want to learn this; Paul didn't want to learn

this. There isn't anyone who wants to learn this, because everybody wants happiness. But the happiness we want can only be fulfilled when the glory of the Cross has been worked out in our lives. But we don't want the glory of the Cross; what we want is the happiness. And the promise of the Cross, and the promise of it coming every day, really must be words that don't have too much meaning. At least this is the way we act.

We come back to these other two readings, and James already has given his life. Peter, so it seems, will give his life now, because the people will do to him what they asked to be done to James, once Herod presents him. But Peter escapes; he escapes this time. And the reason he escapes this time is because the Cross this day is not to take the fullness of his life. It will another day.

And then we go to Paul and he says, "Well, I'm being poured out like a libation." And then he says at the end, "And I am being prepared for the glory. I'm being prepared for the happiness that I always want, and want here and now, and can't get."

There are so many people in life who are sad. They're depressed, upset, distraught. And the reason they are, basically, is because things don't go their way. And every day there is a cross, and every day they don't want the cross. And every day they fight the cross, and every day they don't conquer the cross, and so every day the joy goes out of their living. Somehow they haven't heard—so that they have been able to grow in faith—that this is to be expected. This is part of it; this is the way it is; this is the way it's spelled out; this is its definition.

Perhaps the Book of Proverbs says it well: "Life this side of the grave is a warfare." If one expects, awaits, accepts, moves with the warfare of the day, and one can see in it somehow the plan of the God who says, "I'm giving it to you every day," then there can be joy. There can be a realization that it's worthwhile. He is here; this is his visitation. He's making himself known, and he's inviting me to partake.

But if that desire for happiness has to be spelled out according to my terms—so that anything that comes my way that even bothers me can't be conquered—then, oh! it's depression, despair.

Paul says, "I desire to be dissolved and to move on." The happiness is the desire. The fulfillment is then; the present is now. The resurrection doesn't come until the crucifixion. It was in his life, and it is in ours. This is the way it's supposed to be. This goes over into wee, little things that become crosses that we don't recognize and we want to avoid and do away with.

Let me follow with several little thoughts along these lines, to point out that this is daily living, and we have to catch on and grow in faith, and say, "All right!"

Henri Nouwen says, "When I was young, I so resented interruption to my schedule. But now that I have grown older I have learned that interruption is my schedule." St. Vincent de Paul says, having formed the Daughters of Charity to be people ready for the poor, "If you're praying Vespers, and a poor man knocks at the door, don't say 'I'll see you after Vespers,' just somehow say, 'Jesus is showing his face now, not from the book, but in the person at hand.'"

You know, we're disturbed all the time—I'm talking about human beings, you people back there, too, not just these poor monks. We're disturbed all the time because we're near someone who coughs the way we don't think he should. We're sitting next to somebody who sings off key, so we make sure we won't get near him again if we can possibly have our way. And we fight constantly to oppose what the Lord promises.

Now the people who learn this lesson aren't only those who grow old. Some people grow old, and they grow dumb, it seems. The people who learn this lesson are those who grow old and grow up in faith.

So I say this day has a big challenge for us. There's Peter, that bullhead. There's Paul, who was going to do them all in. And they learned. Now there is that Latin saying, *ex necessi-*

tate faciamus virtutem—we learn virtue when we have to. If we would take the words of the Gospel, and believe them, we would see how much the "have to" is with us every single day.

You know, the world doesn't need people complaining. Dear God, that's what we meet all the time. Look at the Church. Look at the monastery. Look at this. Look at that. Really, I guess, that attitude is saying, "Well, it's not going the way I think it should, and it doesn't fit in with my plan for happiness." But if the Lord's there, and he is, you know what the words are. Spell them out according to your liking. The words are: acceptance, acquiescence, surrender, abandonment. Because Jesus only works out of one context: it's Cross, it's resurrection. And movement with it results in sanctity.

And so it's St. Peter and it's St. Paul. And where are we? Are we on the way? Through their intercession, and with our willingness and God's goodness, we are. Amen.

—June 29, 1996,
the Feast of Saints Peter and Paul.
Renovation Chapel

12.

FAITHFUL WOMAN

My dear friends...

The customs of a culture can bring some clarity to a message. So we look to them. Every adult male Jew who lived within 20 miles of Jerusalem had to attend the Passover feast each year. Every adult male Jew living anywhere in the world had to make every effort to attend at least one Passover celebration in his lifetime. A Jewish boy became an adult at the age of 12. He then moved from being a son of his parents to become a son of the Law. And he had to take upon himself the obligations of the Law.

Mary and Joseph regularly—and Jesus now for the first time—went to the Holy City, to the Temple, for the Passover. The ritual must have fascinated Jesus, because he lingered behind. We offer this as a reason for his staying on.

Joseph must have thought the boy was traveling back with Mary, and vice versa. This was all natural enough. After all, the women started out earlier, the men started out later, they traveled faster, and they would all meet for evening encampment.

A discovery was made at their evening meeting: no Jesus. Upon backtracking, and in discovery, they found Jesus—hearing and asking questions. This was a regular Jewish expression for a student learning from his teachers.

Now, let's get to the key passage with the important message. Customs and culture bring no clarity here. The lesson comes from a woman, from Mary. Mary, with the love and the logic of a mother, says upon discovery of Jesus, "Your father and I have been searching for you in sorrow." Jesus asks, "Why?" With love and logic of another kind, he says, "I have a Father in heaven who has business for me. I'm now an adult—not the son of parents, but the son of the Law."

Mary doesn't understand. Nor does Joseph. And here's the lesson. Mary knows she doesn't have to understand. After all, her inner tutor, the Holy Spirit, didn't teach her to pray, "Be it done unto me according to my understanding," but, rather, "Be it done unto me according to your Word." And when, and however, that Word of yours comes, it's not time for the intellect and its understanding to evaluate, as if the last word belongs within her head. Since her exclusive search in life is for the will of God, she sees this moment and every moment as time for belief.

Elizabeth, early on, is moved by the same inner tutor, the Holy Spirit. Identifying Mary's approach, Elizabeth says, "Blessed is she who believes." Mary believes that all from God is good. And she believes that all is from God. Mary may think Jesus doesn't make sense. But she believes that Jesus doesn't make mistakes; his heart is all love.

When the relationship is *cor ad cor*—heart to heart—it stretches from the sacred to the immaculate. It's Jesus, Mary, communication; and it's the only way to travel. It's revelation, and it's pondering response. Although there's no answer, still on her part there's no complaint.

Today, one of our Fathers is preaching the last day of the Novena to Our Lady of Mount Carmel in Terre Haute. Today, the Sisters from Beech Grove are celebrating Our Lady of Grace. Right here in our exile church, [the temporary "Renovation Chapel"] we're celebrating the feast of Our Lady of Einsiedeln. It doesn't matter the title. But it does matter that she be the teacher, and we be the learners.

And so today we simply say, if we want the meaning of it all, *"Unsere Liebe Frau, bitte für uns"*—Our Dear Lady, whom we love, teach us, for we need to learn. Amen.

—*The Feast of Our Lady of Einsiedeln,*
July 16, 1996.
Theology Chapel

13.

GIRDED UP WITH FAITH

My brothers and sisters, especially today the jubilarians...

Let me tell you a story I have stolen from someone else. In the fifth grade class there were two boys with the name Fred. One Fred, the smaller one, constantly bothered the teacher with his undisciplined antics and his refusal to study. At the first PTA meeting of the year, a polite lady entered the classroom and introduced herself as Fred's mother. Assuming that she was the mother of the other Fred, who was one of her favorite students, the teacher lavishly praised him, said he was a good boy, and a real joy to have in class.

The following morning, little Fred came dashing into the classroom before the other students and threw his arms around the teacher. "Thank you," he sobbed, "for telling my mother I was one of your favorite students, and a joy to have in class." Shocked by his words, but remaining prudently silent, the teacher realized the mistaken identity. "I haven't been good," he said, "but I will be." She softly patted his downcast head, and she turned away in tears. She never revealed that she had thought the nice lady was the mother of the other Fred. Little Fred—let's call him Freddie—was somehow changed from that moment on. He became one of her favorite students, and he was a joy to have in class.

The simple story of the two Freds, in a way, illustrates the parable of the weeds and the wheat in today's Gospel. In real life, weeds don't become wheat. Oh that they would! But in real life, ugliness can be, and often is, changed into beauty. We are naturally proud of the wheat people, and often irritated with the weed people. Like the servants in the story, we

45

might want to pull up the weeds and throw them out. We forget that it's too soon to tell how they will turn out. Many good citizens might have grown up to become criminals had not someone convinced them that they could do better, and had encouraged them to try.

Not only children, but all people, need the affirmation and encouragement of others. The good and the bad are never isolated, but they live side by side through the years. In fact, the good and the bad live inside each one of us. No one becomes a saint in an instant. The seed of sanctity grows slowly, and our God is patience personified. The first reading says so clearly, "You judge with mildness, and with great forbearance you govern us."

The monks we honor today illustrate the point we're trying to make. The monastery is a school; it's a School of the Lord's Service, and from it no one graduates. All the monk does is persevere—persevere to the end of his life for the sake of change, for the sake of becoming better. We call this approach conversion. We speak of it as conversion of life.

The famous chapter 58 in the Holy Rule of our Holy Father Benedict speaks of the one coming as the *"noviter veniens quis ad conversationem"*—the new one who is on the scene for the sake of conversion. The monk is here, as we pray every day in the words of Zachary, to become holy and just in the Lord's sight all the days of his life. The monk is supported by, and put up with by, his brothers. The home of the monk is a house of affirmation, where mutual acceptance is the watchword, because acceptance is what everyone needs.

The monk is taught by the abbot, and the abbot is spoken of by St. Benedict as a *"pius pater,"* a loving father. The monk is taught by the abbot through the abbot's example, by the abbot's instruction, and with correction. And all of this approach is a life that's based on "a little Rule written for beginners." And in this life the years pass; every little Fred changes. And when a quarter or a half of a century passes, then we pause, and we note a few of these changes. Such a day is good for all of us. It honors the jubilarians, it gives us all hope, and it brings joy into our hearts.

Now, Br. John. Are you here, Br. John? Br. John for many, many years was the sacristan. Then Br. John for a number of years was the infirmarian. He dealt with the sick. Then Br. John was sacristan again. Br. John is a friend of Br. Benedict's. They're famous for their weekend walks. I'm sorry we don't have tape recordings of their talks. Br. John is a lover of cars; he has all kinds of cars he collects. Br. John for his jubilee present from the abbot is going to get a ride in the abbot's new car. Not too long ago I was at a particular place and they gave me a calendar, and the calendar had pictures of all the old-time cars. I gave it to Br. John, and he was so happy. Br. John has carried an affliction for years. We all carry afflictions; his is visible. But with it all Br. John has been so pleasant. Br. John can be seen at the bulletin board in the evening after Compline, looking at the menu for the next morning's breakfast. Br. John never misses a coffee break, and Br. John has eaten tons of chocolates. Br. John is a good monk.

Fr. Camillus. Fr. Camillus is probably more like little Fred than the rest, and his family knows this well. In his old age now, Fr. Camillus has taken to writing his memoirs. I've picked them up several times, and I would say when he was a kid he must have been a devil. Fr. Camillus for many, many years was known as the little brother of Fr. Gerard. But Fr. Camillus has come into his own. Fr. Camillus is a sociologist. For many years he was an infirmarian. Fr. Camillus taught our class in what was called fifth theology, and he had a lot of practical things to tell us about working in a parish. Fr. Camillus for a long time was the pastor of the big St. Benedict's in Evansville. Fr. Camillus is now pastor of a parish which could be called heaven on earth. It's St. Henry, Indiana. Fr. Camillus is an advisor to the abbot and to the community: he's a counselor. Fr. Camillus is someone who, because of God's will, has to get to Wyoming every summer. It just seems that the summer calls him to the West. Fr. Camillus is a good monk.

Fr. Cyril. Fr. Cyril is beloved of his students. Fr. Cyril taught math for a long time. Probably one of the biggest donations we have gotten, or at least it's promised because of a good teacher, is a gift that comes our way because of Fr. Cyril. It's given by a man who went on to become a Doctor in Mathematics. Fr. Cyril was an Army man. He traveled the globe. We got letters from him from all over the world. I think sometimes they weren't written at camp, but at places that he happened to visit. Fr. Cyril one time wrote a letter to the community from Korea, I think, and he said, "It's the first time I haven't met Sisters who have asked, 'Do you know Fr. Lambert?'" Fr. Cyril is a great preacher. He's a kind confessor. Fr. Cyril was at one time pastor of St. Benedict's. Fr. Cyril has done extended parish work in Tennessee and Arizona. Fr. Cyril works for the development office, and right now he's interviewing the old monks in the monastery—and [pointing to himself] the interviewing is coming down to some of us— and he's gaining a lot of important information for our history. Fr. Cyril writes the *Monkly Tydings* for our in-house *Community Bulletin*. He has a very kind way of poking fun at all of us. Fr. Cyril often says, "There are no more characters in the monastery." As long as Fr. Cyril's alive, that won't be true. Fr. Cyril is patient in suffering. Fr. Cyril dearly loves his family, especially his brother, Patrick. Fr. Cyril is a great friend of Fr. Gavin, and Fr. Gavin is a great friend to him. They exercise and do therapy together every day. Fr. Cyril is a good monk.

And now we have covered three who have given 50 years of their lives to our community and to our way of life. We come to the next three. We might blame Fr. Conrad for them. Fr. Conrad was their novice master, and he's right here in the front row.

The first one we come to is Fr. Tobias. I taught Fr. Tobias in third year high school. It might be better to say that in third year high school he was in my class. Fr. Tobias is an accomplished musician. They tell me this—and I wouldn't know what it means, but I have a tendency to believe them when they tell me things—that Fr. Tobias has perfect pitch. Fr. Tobias is just back now from the Oregon Catholic Press. He spent ten days singing, singing, singing. And he spent ten days singing, singing, singing what he wrote, he wrote, he wrote. CDs will be available soon. You'll all want them. Fr. Tobias is the abbot's secretary, his administrative assistant. When I look good, it's because Fr. Tobias makes me look good; and Fr. Tobias enjoys doing it. Fr. Tobias is a master of detail. Very, very little escapes him. Fr. Tobias is a French and a Spanish teacher, but he can't teach now because he has to do something else. Fr. Tobias is kind to everyone; he has patience that's unbelievable. Fr. Tobias is gentle and witty, and he's clever in the very best sense. Fr. Tobias is a good monk.

(They told me to talk a long time because they don't know what to do with you before dinner. You'll know what to do at dinner, won't you?)

We come to Br. Hugh. Br. Hugh, for whatever reason, is often spoken of as "The Brother." Br. Hugh presently is helping very much as one of the steady breakfast cooks. He does a great job. Br. Hugh has had lots of jobs. He is featured in the newspapers more than the abbot, and it's all in connection with rabbits. Br. Hugh runs the Abbey Rabbitry and Hedgehog Inn. Br. Hugh is practically a shadow of himself; in the last number of months he's lost 36½ pounds. If you see him, and wonder who he is, well, he's the new Br. Hugh. Br. Hugh makes a lot of coffee in the calefactory. When he comes in, usually the pot is empty, and he very kindly prepares for those who are coming after him. Br. Hugh is from St. Benedict's in Evansville. When he was younger he worked with the Little Sisters. He was so fascinated by them, he wanted to join them. But they told him he couldn't. And he said, "If I can't be a Little Sister, then I'll be a big brother." It so happens that I gave the retreat to Br. Hugh's class when he was in the eighth grade. Every so often he tells me I taught him about the birds and the bees. But I think the rabbits have taught him much more. Br. Hugh is not one who is afraid to ask for permissions; he asks them endlessly. And Br. Hugh gets a lot of what he asks for. But one thing I had to refuse him: He wanted to know if the hedgehogs and the rabbits could come to this celebration, and I told him they would change the scene too much. Br. Hugh is a good monk.

Fr. Jeremy. Fr. Jeremy is a musician, a singer, a preacher, a parish man. He's an organizer. I taught Fr. Jeremy in first year high school. Fr. Jeremy is one who is forever sought out. People are calling: "Can he give this talk?" "Can he do this work?" "Can he be stationed here?" A little bit of advice I'd give Fr. Jeremy in front of all of you: He ought to get over his bashfulness. Fr. Jeremy is a good monk.

For monks, the Gospel is our guide. For monks, we are to be girded up with faith. For the monks of Saint Meinrad, Our Lady of Einsiedeln is our Mother. Benedict is our father; Meinrad is our patron. And these six monks are our brothers. We love them; we're proud of them. Some days we're more proud than other days. They make our day and our life happy, and we hope that we do the same for them.

May we all continue to keep "the little Rule" of Benedict, to keep it better, to be together to pray, to be together to enjoy our meals, to be together to help each other in need. All we're doing is hastening toward our heavenly home. And in our heavenly home there will be jubilees forever and ever. Amen.

—July 21, 1996,
on the Jubilees of Profession.
Theology Chapel

14.

LIVING A WAY THAT WORKS

Brother Brendan and Brother Adrian...

For a few moments I want to talk to you as a *pius pater*, a loving father. You desire to follow Christ more closely and imitate him more nearly. And that desire of yours will be spelled out through the vows you will pronounce. For a moment, with you, I'd like to look at each one of those vows.

There is the vow of poverty, wherein you give up, and wherein you gain. You give up all, and you gain a hundred-fold here, and you gain eternal life. As your life goes on, by the grace of this vow, you will find, as Pope John Paul II says, "God is the true wealth of your human hearts." By this vow you will be free from possessions, and you will be free for God. Our Holy Father Benedict reminds us that we must root out what in our way of life is a vice: private ownership. In our tradition, we hear the expression *quidquid monachus acquirit, monasterium acquirit*—whatever the monk acquires, the monastery acquires. We're well taken care of; you don't have to worry about that.

Just a few years ago I had the great blessing of having cancer surgery, as you know. I like to talk about that. I had the great blessing of knowing chemotherapy once a week for a year. And I also had a blessing which a lot of you wouldn't know—and you'll know that blessing some other way: I did-n't have to open up a bill; all I did was pass those bills on to those who pay.

You give up, but you get more than you ever give up.

There's the vow of chastity. That vow tells everyone who

gets to know you that you believe in the life that is to come. You already by that vow will belong to God in a very special way. You still belong to your family, you belong to the Church, you belong to this family, which is Saint Meinrad. And in this family you will learn to love your abbot and love your brethren, and they will learn to love you.

In the document on religious life, there is a quote that runs, "The greatest protection for the vow of chastity is the practice of fraternal charity." We voted for you because we love you, and we are your very special family. In giving up, you'll really gain more.

There's the vow of obedience. Our Holy Father Benedict speaks that in and through obedience we don't even have our own body under our charge. This vow you make by free choice. This vow is a vow that enables you—and I say it this way on purpose—to walk according to someone else's judgment. But that judgment comes from a proven way of life that will lead you to God. As Our Holy Father Benedict says so well, *"Dura et aspera quae itur ad Deum"*—"It's the difficult things, the hard things, that lead us to the God whom we so love."

I have given a few retreats in my life, you may know that. I remember one time talking to a particular religious who said she had an obedience that was so easy. And then she had an obedience that was so difficult. After talking for a while, I assured her that the obedience which she considered so easy was really agreement. Obedience is always difficult, and it's meant to be. But it's a proof of love of the Christ whom you choose to follow. St. Francis de Sales says so simply, "The superior may sin in commanding. The subject will never, ever sin in obeying."

And then we go on beyond these three vows, and we come to that beautiful vow of stability. This means that by this vow you pledge yourself to the life and the work of this community. For you, somehow, as for all of us who belong, Saint Meinrad, Indiana, here in southern Indiana, is the center of our world. You belong to all of us by this vow, and we belong to you. It's not always easy. I keep saying that.

We have a school song that goes like this (don't worry, I won't sing it): "Wherever we are, be it near, be it far, from Saint Meinrad, our dear alma mater." There may be moments when you would like to sing: "Wherever we are just so long as it's far…" But all these people here know what that's like in the vocation that is theirs.

There is that other vow, conversion of life. That's the reason we think of our life, as Our Holy Father Benedict says, as a School of the Lord's Service. We're learning. We're changing. It's not merely information; it's formation. In this school no one graduates.

We know that the Lord God sees us with a double vision. He sees us for what we are, but he also sees us for what we can become. And because we are interested in conversion of life, we desire to be corrected. We want our abbot to give us a good word. We want our brethren to tell us how to change. Especially, though, we want our abbot and our brethren to teach us through their way of life.

All of us, as St. Augustine says, are *peccatores in re, sancti in spe*—we're sinners in reality, but we're saints in hope. As the same Augustine says, each one of us is *simul justus et peccator*—each one of us is a sinner, but each one of us is just.

And so I say to you, you're entering a proven way of life. It works, if you let it. We can look at saints galore who have passed through the way of life you are entering into fully. And we know by now so well that there is no other success other than sanctity.

And so I now say to you two specifically, Brother Brendan and Brother Adrian: You want us, we want you. Let us now seal our bond in the name of God.

—August 15, 1996,
at Solemn Vow Exhortation.
College Chapel

15.

Four Guys Who Graduated

Within the last few months we have known some significant dates. I recount them: April 6; June 19; August 28; September 18. These dates refer to four monks, one who was born in New Albany, Indiana, one who was born in Ashley, Pennsylvania, one who was born in New Riegel, Ohio, and one who was born in Indianapolis, Indiana. These men were born in 1916, 1915, 1930 and 1906. These men: Fr. Marcellus, Br. Methodius, Br. René, Fr. Dunstan.

These important dates were the dates of their death. These monks made their stability here at Saint Meinrad for the sake of conversion of life. They came here to our School of the Lord's Service. During their stay here, they were invited to keep death daily before their eyes. They were invited, further, to desire death with all spiritual longing. They weren't the exception; this is what Our Holy Father Benedict invites each monk to do. They participated in the prayer, the desire, of our *Pius Pater*, Benedict, that together the Lord Jesus would bring us all to everlasting life. They were here professed for 59, for 37, for 42, for 68 years. The Lord gave them a burden; the Lord made it light. And their burden is now lifted, whereas ours isn't. We pray for them. We pray to them. And the Lord God knows what to do with that prayer.

Remember Marcellus. He was the Prince. Prince Marcellus. You remember Methodius. He was the locksmith. Remember René. How shall we remember René? For this moment let's say he was the laundry manager. Remember Fr. Dunstan. Fr. Dunstan was famous, on a day like this when we're all dressed in black and there's no blessing, for having started it, and then erased it.

They were here, but they've gone; and we're here now. And how long we'll be here, we don't know. But what we know for sure is that someday we'll be gone. And so, while we're here for conversion of life at Saint Meinrad, it might be good for us to keep death daily before our eyes, and to learn to desire it with all spiritual longing.

You remember Fr. Alaric. One day after some of Fr. Alaric's antics, I said to him, "You will be in purgatory until the world ends." And he said to me, "Just pray that you get there." Maybe today we ought to pray that we get there.

This past summer Fr. Aelred, Fr. Nathaniel and I visited our confrere, Fr. Benedict. In his very simple—very simple— rectory, sort of like a hermitage, on the wall Fr. Benedict had a quote which attracted me. I asked him to write it down. He put it on this card [with an image of St. Benedict on the front], and maybe today, because of what we celebrate, maybe today it has lots of meaning. It goes like this: "To love is to be free to die, to leave all things unfinished, to go to God without regretting the interruption."

For Fr. Dunstan and Br. René and Fr. Marcellus and Br. Methodius, we pray. But for ourselves let us pray, and let us ask them and all our departed brethren, to pray for us, to keep it all in focus. And if we desire death with spiritual longing, our vision will be at least 20/20. Amen.

—November 2, 1996,
the Feast of All Souls.
Renovation Chapel

16.

EMMANUEL

When we ask them how we are to explain mystery, they tell us: "Tell it as a story, as a parable." They tell us, though, that every explanation limps. Somehow, sometimes, the story tells only half of it. And, if so, then we must tell the rest of it after the story's over, or we must tell a second story or parable.

With these confused thoughts, let's approach this holy night. Let's do so with a parable. Let it be the first half of the story. It's a stolen one.

It was Christmas Eve. And the man's wife and children were getting ready to go to church. He wasn't going. "I simply can't understand what Christmas is all about, this claim that God became a man," he told his wife.

It had been snowing all day, and it was beginning to snow harder as the man's family drove off to the church without him. He drew a chair up to the fireplace, and he began to read his newspaper. Suddenly, there was a thudding sound at the kitchen window. Investigating, he found a flock of birds in the backyard. They had been caught in the storm, and in a desperate search for shelter, were trying to fly through the kitchen window.

He was a kind man, so he tried to think of something that he could do so that the birds wouldn't freeze. "The barn!" he thought. The barn would provide a nice shelter. He put on his coat and his overshoes and he tramped through the snow to the barn. He opened the door wide, and he turned on the light. But the birds didn't come in.

"Food! Food will bring them in!" he thought. So he hurried to the house for bread crumbs, which he then sprinkled on the snow to make a trail into the barn. But the birds ignored the crumbs, and continued to flock around helplessly in the snow.

He tried now to shoo them into the barn by walking around and waving his arms. They scattered in every direction, except into the warm, lighted barn. "They find me a strange and terrifying creature," he said to himself. "And I can't think of any way to let them know that they can trust me." Puzzled and dismayed, he pondered this thought. "If only I could be a bird myself for a moment, I could lead them to safety. If only I could be a bird myself."

Just then, the church bells began to ring, pealing the glad tidings of Christmas. The man stood silent for a minute, and then he sank to his knees in the snow. "Now I think I understand," he whispered as he lifted his gaze to the sky. "Now I see why you had to become a man."

Well, God didn't have to become a man. But he did. And thereby he saves us, not as a remote, detached, isolated, majestic God. But he saves us as one seeing things with eyes like unto ours, and feeling things with emotions we know, and thinking things with a mind that is made as are ours. He saves us as one experiencing temptation, according to the makeup of what our nature allows. There is one big difference between him and us: He does it all better than we can; he does it without sin.

Now he is as we are, and the parable has gotten us this far. So let us go on to the other half of the story, the second parable, the one limping with mystery: Now we are as he must be.

And how does, or how can, or how will, the second story spell that out? Well, Isaiah has urged us, "His authority shall grow continually." Till with Paul we could be able to say, "No longer I who live." Leo the Great told us, "Remember your dignity. Now you share God's own nature." And Leo warns, "Do not return to your former faith condition." Paul, again, now to Titus: He says that we are to live lives that are self controlled, that are upright.

But maybe the word is that we are to live lives that are Godly, because we're involved in what we call *O Admirabile Commercium*, that wonderful exchange. In a certain real sense we say it has begun again. The *Catechism of the Catholic Church* captures it: "Only when Christ is formed in us will the mystery of Christmas be fulfilled in us."

The rest of the story—call it parable—willy nilly, we write, you and I. He has become one of us. We write the rest with our lives. And if we don't, then the night is historically Christ's alone. Period. And we merely admire and say, "What a beautiful baby."

In this celebration, the choice is once again ours. This can truly be for us, with his help and our willing involvement in this mystery, an *Anno Domino*, a Year of Our Lord. We ask very simply, "What are we going to do?" If we're given another year, will we be more like the One who became one like us? Or will it be pomp, splendor, and just a passing night?

Pray God—pray God—we do as we should, because Jesus did as God chose.

—December 25, 1996,
Christmas Midnight Mass.
Renovation Chapel

17.

A Place For Us

It is the Hebrew Scriptures which picture for us Elijah ascending in a chariot. The New Testament just now tells us that Jesus ascended.

There's a here... there's a hereafter... and they're for everyone. A dramatic going to the hereafter is extremely exceptional. But the going to the hereafter is without question. It happens. And it's for each and every one of us in time. We speak of going up as the goal. We contrast it with going down; that's not our goal. How to live here, what to expect hereafter, is knowledge that has to come from Christ. And that's simply because every good thing has to come from Christ, since he is the source from which it flows.

The feast, the readings today, are meant to be our guide on these issues. Readings are never more powerful than when contexted in the feast they are to celebrate and to explain. To explain how we are to live here, Acts tells us, "Be my witnesses to the ends of the earth." And so we are to live here as witnesses. Ephesians tells us, "When he ascended he gave gifts for the building up of the body." And so we are to build up the body here, with our gifts. Mark tells us, "Those gifts, to be taken to all the world, are to center on proclamation of the Good News, that Jesus is Lord." And so here we are to be witnesses who build up the Church by proclaiming Jesus as Lord of the here and the hereafter.

To explain what we are to expect hereafter, the Book of Acts says, "Don't expect knowledge now. It's not for us to know what the hereafter is." We, on the other hand, to strengthen our point, add the text, "We can't know because eye has not seen and ear has not heard"—at least ours haven't. We add to the importance of the hereafter by looking at the text that asks, "What does it profit if we gain everything, but lose …?"

Three people, who recently were here, and are now in the hereafter, now know what the hereafter is like. For their eye has seen, and their ear has heard, and is hearing. But let us be reminded that they're not sharing that knowledge with us. For our not knowing, except through personal experience, still binds. From where I sit, I say that these three people were witnesses, who with their gifts built up their world by proclaiming Jesus as Lord of the here and the hereafter.

The first of these people lived in downtown St. Meinrad, Indiana. I met him in 1993. We began cancer treatments together. I kept in touch with him. I learned that he lived in the little white house near the Abbey Press gate and that for years he worked at the Press. I learned he had a big family, a loving family. He was always thrilled when we met; he was delighted when I visited him. He was cheerful, and he was prayerful. He died recently. I went to the funeral home the night before to view him, because a scheduled meeting kept me from the funeral. His witnessing, his building up, his proclaiming that Jesus is Lord, came from his being a good husband and father, and from being patient in suffering. From where I sit, I would say he was a just man. I'm speaking of Erwin Bertke.

The second person who was recently here, and is now in the hereafter, lived in Indianapolis. I met her father last year. He was a presenter at a development seminar. We discovered that I knew his parents. His daughter died last week. She was only 10 years old. She was diagnosed with cancer at an extremely early age, around the age of two, and she had endless surgeries. Her father kept in contact with me since our meeting. I prayed for her. Her name was Emily Seiler. It so happens I was confirming in Indianapolis when she died. I went to St. Matthew Parish where she was laid out. Kids from the school were all over the place; some, with tears, told me that she often talked to them about dying, telling them that dying was good. On this day when I saw them... they were wondering about that. Emily's mother and dad told me that she taught them how to live. And she showed them how to die.

The church scene on that afternoon was awesome. There were children expressing every mood our makeup is capable of. They were sitting, they were staring, they were dancing. Emily Seiler witnessed; she built up the Church by proclaiming that Jesus is Lord. She did it by being the simple, accepting little girl that she was. "Out of the mouths of babes and sucklings ..."

The third person who recently died lived in Pittsburgh, and died in Miami. He was my brother. He was like a father to me, because my father died at age 42, leaving eight of us. He, Matt, was my oldest brother. He was drafted into the service while still a senior in high school. He never married. He took care of us younger ones, and he stayed with my mother. You wouldn't think that he and I were related: He was always gentle and kind, and this came in handy living with my mother. Suffice it to say that she and I were alike.

My brother Matt gave his life for us, and he gave his body to science when God called him home. He witnessed; he built up the Church by using his God-given gifts for others. He learned early on that Jesus is Lord.

Now, for us, for you and for me, hereafter isn't here yet. And I bet that we won't go out in glory like Elijah, Jesus or Benedict. I imagine we probably will leave here somewhat like Erwin, Emily and Matt. But today, the feast tells us, because there is an Ascension, and because there is a Jesus, he has prepared a place for us, a place for you, a place for me. We should ask the grace of this feast, so that we may be witnesses building up the Body of Christ. Wherever our vocation has called us, we should use our gifts, and we should use them in such a way that we may say, here and hereafter: Jesus Christ is Lord. Amen.

—May 8, 1997,
Ascension Thursday.
Renovation Chapel

18.

TRINITY

Fr. Michael, Fr. Richard, Fr. Stephen, and everybody else...

Even though the mystery of the Trinity, the mystery of the Triune God, the mystery of God as Three Persons is the cornerstone of our Christian religion, one is forced to conclude with theologians like Karl Rahner that it plays a modest role in the conscious spiritual life of most Catholics. This isn't really strange, when we recall that mystery is—and is supposed to be—only one sided. This means, then, that the mystery of the Trinity is not incomprehensible to the Three Persons, Father, Son and Holy Spirit. So to speak, it's the ordinary experience which they are. There's nothing at all strange to them about it; it's not really mystery to them. The one-sidedness making the mystery touches us, not them. The mystery of the Trinity doesn't totally baffle us, but it does intrigue us—and it eludes us.

Its ongoing understanding will move our way as we move its way in the fullness of life to come. In fact, we will spend our life in eternity in wonder and in awe of the Most Holy Trinity. We will never fully rise to complete understanding of the Godhead, because to do so would make us equal to God. And this is impossible.

St. Columban speaks about the Trinity. First he asks, "Who then is God?" And he answers, "He is Father, Son and Holy Spirit." Then he counsels, "Do not look for any further answers concerning God. As the depths of the seas are invisible to human sight, so the Godhead of the Trinity is found to be beyond the grasp of human understanding." And then he again counsels, "Just believe."

If the mystery of the Trinity now plays a modest role in our conscious spiritual life, when we enter eternal life it will be our consuming passion. Let's look to why and how this comes about. Why will it go from a modest role to a consuming passion?

Well, the Father sent the Son from his Trinity home to ultimately bring us to that same Trinity home. Jesus says, "Where I am, you also will be." How is this to come about, that we move from modest role to consuming passion? In and through the priesthood, and the work of the priesthood. To the first priests, and to every priest since the first priests, Jesus says, "As the Father has sent me, so I send you." The work of the priest is Christ's work. His work is the work of the priest. All this through what we now call ordination. The commands, "Take and eat, take and drink; do this in remembrance of me," enable priests to make Christ present.

Christ gives them this power through the sacraments, beginning with, "Go therefore and make disciples of all nations, baptizing them in the name of the Father, and of the Son and of the Holy Spirit." This trinitarian homecoming, which we will know again, comes our way through the power of repeated forgiveness, for the sake of repeated beginning. Jesus says, "Whose sins you shall forgive, they are forgiven them." And we know this is 70 times seven, and it's not merely 490 times.

Priesthood enables and facilitates our entrance to trinitarian life. The powers of the priesthood are for that purpose, so that as legitimate heirs of Christ we can truly cry out, "Abba, Father."

Now, who are priests, and what are they like? Well, let's name Peter and Paul, Andrew and Thomas. We know snippets of their personalities from the Sacred Scripture; we get ideas of what they're like.

But now today we have monks featured. They're priests, and their names are Joachim, Michael, Richard and Stephen. Why are they priests? It's a good question; the answer is not evident in the one-sidedness of mystery which is ours.

What priest has not often asked himself, "Why me?" And how many other people have sometimes asked about them, "Why them?" We know a little bit, as I said, about Peter, Paul, Andrew and Thomas. Today let's say a public word about Joachim and Michael and Richard and Stephen.

Fr. Joachim is a priest for 60 years. He lives at Tickfaw, Louisiana. He comes from a family of six children, and they're all religious. If you say to Fr. Joachim, "You come from a holy family," he says, "No, it takes six of us to make a good one." Fr. Joachim is a joyful person and a clever person. He's a kind person. In 1951 I was sliding down the banister in St. Bede Hall. Fr. Joachim was the dean. He was at the bottom of the steps. As I landed, he said to me, "Bill, if you ever see anyone sliding down the banister, you'd better tell him he's not allowed." Fr. Joachim taught Latin, and he had all kinds of jingles. One I remember so well: "After *si, nisi, num* and *ne,* the prefix *ali* falls away." He taught constantly like that. What does Fr. Joachim do now? He rides the tractor. The six in his family are all gathered together in a monastery in Louisiana. Fr. Joachim, however, is always the monk and the priest.

Now, Fr. Michael. His head goes down [as I say his name]… and there will be good reason for it! Fr. Michael comes from Indianapolis, and now he works in Indianapolis. He's a priest 60 years. Fr. Michael taught Canon Law in the seminary for a long time. You'd never know it; he has a doctorate in Canon Law. Fr. Michael was a prefect in that part of the institution which in those days was called the major seminary. Fr. Michael took his turn as prior, the second superior in the house. Fr. Michael always was, and always is, kind. And he is laid back; we wondered if he'd be with us on time. I remember Kate Smith—I'm sure Fr. Michael's old enough to remember Kate Smith—and I liked her version of *I Left My Heart in San Francisco.* I think Fr. Michael left part of his heart in Peru; he was there for a long time. Recently Fr. Michael was almost dead after his terrible car accident. But look at him now. Fr. Michael is an adjustable fellow: He was the oblate director for an amount of time, and now he's the Associate at St. John's in Indianapolis. Recently I was in Indianapolis to give a talk to a group of Disciples of Christ. I thought, "Thank God, there won't be anybody here that I know and so I can say anything I want; it can be a repeat." I looked out, and there was Fr. Michael, with a whole slew of oblates! Fr. Michael is a pious man; he has a tender devotion to the Blessed Mother. Fr. Michael is sort of like an expression he uses, "Say, you big horse." Fr. Michael's a big horse. But Fr. Michael is always the monk and the priest.

(Aren't you glad there aren't twelve?!)

Fr. Richard. Fr. Richard is an earthy man, the salt of the earth. Of course, he's ordained only 50 years. Fr. Richard is a botanist, and he's a biologist. Fr. Richard is a tough guy, but he's a sweet guy. Fr. Richard was the director of the oblate house, when we had a high school for young men studying to be brothers. He was a prefect and the vice rector in our School of Theology. Fr. Richard was the subprior, and he was the brother instructor. Fr. Richard is calm, cool, collected. Fr. Richard is the type you can always give a job, when it's a tough job and hardly anyone else could do it. Fr. Richard knows how to have a good time. (Did I get more of a noise on that?) Fr. Richard is never showy. Fr. Richard is presently Administrator at Lourdes Parish in Indianapolis. Who knows what's coming next? If I know, I'm not saying. But Fr. Richard is always the monk. He's always the priest.

Well, Fr. Stephen, your time has come. Fr. Stephen was a bit older coming in; he had a life out there we don't know too much about. He tells us he was a construction boss. We know the boss part of it's true! When Fr. Stephen came, he worked as a novice helping to build the guest house. We hear about it all the time; it seems everybody from around our time helped Fr. Stephen over there. But I didn't. And please don't ask for his version of why I didn't. Fr. Stephen right now is the unofficial "clerk of the works." He's out there on that building site. He's moving around everywhere with the workers; he's up on the scaffold. You know how you can take 'em out of it but you can't take it out of 'em—I mean the boss part? Fr. Stephen was a brother for many years. When he was at St. Charles, which is now Prince of Peace, he got a strong call to priesthood. One thing you have to say about Fr. Stephen is that he has guts. He struggled, he worked, he stayed with it, he was ordained. He spent a number of years at St. Benedict's in Evansville, and he developed Irish Cop stories. When he would preach on Sunday, the Irish Cop first had something to say in and through him. Fr. Stephen at one time had severe heart problems. He didn't die; he has to live to repent. Fr. Stephen is now a chaplain to the elderly Sisters at Ferdinand, and he offers comfort and consolation to co-workers who are ill, and to their families who have problems. Once he became a priest, this monk remained a priest.

We're connected to the mystery of the Trinity by the mystery of the priesthood. We have three here and one there who were called to be an *alter Christus*, like Christ in a special way. They're the monk-priests Joachim, Michael, Richard and Stephen. May they lead us and many others by their ministry to the fullness of the Trinity, beyond our one-sidedness, to the home where we all will be one. That we all may be one, as Thou, Father, in me, and I in Thee, and may we know this all through the power of the Holy Spirit, forever and ever. Amen.

—May 25, 1997,
the Feast of the Holy Trinity.
Theology Chapel

19.

PRAY FOR ME

Tobit describes what were his acts of charity, which once got him into prison. They were acts of charity that really had a New Testament approach. He gave food to the hungry, he clothed the naked, he buried the dead. At a particular Pentecost feast, home from prison with his family, he invited the poor from the by-ways. He sent his son Tobias out to be his spokesperson.

Tobias came back and said that one of their own had been strangled, murdered. So Tobit left the banquet and went to bury him. His neighbors laughed at Tobit. They said, "You were once put into prison for burying the dead. Won't you ever learn?"

Tobit learned not what they suggested, but what leaders need to learn. There are times in the life of every leader when no good deed goes unpunished. The leader has to pay for the good he does. If he is a leader, he doesn't give up. He doesn't gloss over the demands of his job, no matter the cost, because he's a leader, and God is with him.

Mark's parable exposes the divine irony of God. In a foolhardy way he sends his own son to tenant farmers, who are proven recalcitrant. Are these tenant farmers so badly disposed that they will kill even his son? Yes, they are, and yes, they do. Here's a picture of the Father delivering up his only Son for us, while we were still sinners. From this story we are to learn that the leader, to be leader, must lay down his own life. There is no other way.

Two years after election as leader, as abbot, I need to note and remember today's Scripture messages: No good deed goes unpunished. Laying down one's life is required.

Our Holy Father Benedict says, *"Abbatem suum sincera et humili caritate diligant"*—"Let the monks love their abbot with a sincere and humble heart." And so I say to you, because I am your abbot and you are to love me, and you want me to be a leader with God as my guide: Pray for me. Pray for me specifically that the Prayer of St. Aelred that I pray for you every day may ring true. This is what I pray every day: "You know my heart, Lord, that whatever you have given to your servant, I desire to spend it wholly on them, and to consume it all in their service."

Pray for me. I pray for you. God will supply whatever is lacking. With the Gospel as our guide, and Benedict as our tradition, we will move forward, so that in all things God may be glorified.

—June 2, 1997.
The second anniversary of
Archabbot Lambert's election as abbot.
Renovation Chapel

20.

THE CROSS STANDS

My brothers & sisters...

Peter says, "You are the Messiah." Jesus says, "Yes, I am, and it's my Father who has revealed this to you." It's the highlight of the Gospel account. But the next five verses of Matthew are so much more telling: "The Messiah is the Suffering Servant," says Jesus. "And my disciples must share in that suffering," says Jesus. "That suffering is called a daily cross, and we're in it together, without exception," says Jesus.

After the definition of the Messiah as Suffering Servant, Peter says, "No, no! It can't be!" After his, "No, no," Jesus says, "Yes, yes. For what's mine is yours. Unjust suffering will be for both of us and all my followers."

From the Gospel to the first reading, the "Yes, yes" of the follower's suffering is shown because it's Peter's turn; the prediction is spelled out. Herod has killed James with the sword. The people like it. Peter is next; it's just a matter of time. Imprisonment, planned by Herod, until death, similar to that of James, is now Peter's lot. But, instead, this time an angel appears, and Peter's freedom is secured. Herod and the people are thwarted. Peter explains, "I am sure that the Lord has sent his angel and rescued me from the hands of Herod and from all that the people were expecting."

Now we turn the page, and we go to the second reading. It's Paul's turn. He's in a prison in Rome, writing to Timothy, directing him for his task in Ephesus, saying that the Gospel is worth suffering for. Paul's life is presently where his mouth is; he's authentic. He's proving that the Gospel, who is Jesus, is worth suffering for. Paul talks of being rescued from the lion's mouth this time, and adds that the Lord will rescue him from every evil attack.

The experiences of Peter and Paul, thus far spoken of, were preliminary to their martyrdoms, from which there was no rescue. Then there was only deliverance to their call. Tradition has the martyrdoms of Peter and Paul taking place in Rome. Literally, the Cross became Peter's, but an upside-down version. But death by martyrdom also came to Paul, by the sword, around the year 66.

Peter's and Paul's approach to accepting each previous cross merited them the crown of their final cross. If we die with Christ, we will rise with Christ. Peter and Paul's lives spell out how to become perfect, how to become saints, as they now are in heaven. As the *Catechism of the Catholic Church* so adroitly says, "The way of perfection passes by way of the Cross."

No bloody martyrdom for us, so it seems. But we can't say, "No cross," because there isn't such a thing as crossless Christianity. Such would be a contradiction in terms. How we handle our crosses, how we embrace them, determines if we will join in the long line of saints after the primaries—Peter and Paul, or not.

Those who can't stand injustice done them, those who rebel against unfairness coming their way, those who are always ready to retaliate in vengeance if someone gets them, belong to the unhappy group—and so large it is—forever asking, "Why, why?" to every pain visiting them. They're filled with anger. They're never happy. Things are always wrong. They don't know what to do. And they are light years away from the Christians (the real ones) who in the same or similar situations don't ask, "Why, why?" but ask, "What do you want me to learn now from this, Lord?" This group—and it's small—desires to be like Jesus, from whose mouth came no word of regret or self-pity in any and every injustice he suffered.

No one has to tell us how to live when things go our

way. But somebody has to tell us that life is worth living when they don't. And that someone is Christ, and it's Christ alone. Christ the Messiah, who is the Suffering Servant, into whose life and cross Peter and Paul entered and reveled. *Crux stat et orbis revolvitur*—the cross stands and the world revolves around it.

Like Peter, we are to learn that our "No, no" is to become Christ's "Yes, yes." Like Paul, we are to pray, "May I glory in nothing, save in the Cross of Our Lord Jesus Christ." The learning time is now. And it's the learning time for you and for me. The learning time is right now. The question is: Will we learn? Only you and I and Jesus have that answer. Amen.

—June 29, 1997,
the Feast of Saints Peter and Paul.
Renovation Chapel

21.

GOING UP BY
GOING DOWN

The Father's will, which Jesus comes to do—the Father's will for Jesus—is to raise up on the last day all who come to him. Those who have come here to our monastery in the past, and those who come now, at least implicitly hope(d) to be raised up on the last day. This is the basic reason for coming to Jesus here, or anywhere, and at any time.

The last-day raising is the goal for living. Our Holy Father Benedict says, "Desire death with all spiritual longing." One does this desiring by keeping death daily before one's eyes, and letting it influence everything the monk does. Learning this is learning wisdom. It's the buried treasure we search for in life, before our own burial stages itself.

Today, in our commemoration of deceased abbots, monks and benefactors, we're reminded by the lives of real people that this lesson is extremely important. It's wisdom supreme.

Abbot (and first Archabbot) Ignatius of Saint Meinrad had to learn—and we pray he did—*Humilitate ascendere*, his coat of arms. You go up by going down. Being humble is what exalts you. This view, which can come only from eternity (the world can't stand it), which we're invited to use as our only daily standard of judgment, demands the approach we refer to in reference to Abbot Ignatius. It's a must.

Fr. Fintan Baltz had to learn—and we pray he did—that his consecrated, priestly hands took on new meaning from the dirt he worked with for years. For his life was spent in the abbey garden. His words still echo for those of us who can hear him in memory, "I've got to get the kale in!" His concern was so much for the garden.

John Berry, the financial genius for many a religious community, and a great help for ours at Abbot Gabriel's request, moved away from his personal wealth to his last days spent peacefully with the Little Sisters of the Poor.

Let's not let the lesson of this insignificant liturgical commemoration be lost on us. As far as the east is from the west, so far are his ways from ours. Jesus says, "My message from my Father is to raise them up on the last day."

Abbot Ignatius, Fr. Fintan, John Berry, pray for us, from the wisdom which is now fully yours. Amen.

—July 17, 1997,
Commemoration of Deceased Abbots,
Monks & Benefactors of Saint Meinrad.
Renovation Chapel

22.

WHAT ANIMAL WOULD YOU LIKE TO BE?

My sisters and brothers...

Lambs. Sheep. Shepherd. Flock. There are so many of these words in the Hebrew Scriptures, in the New Testament, in the Holy Rule of St. Benedict, that they cannot be dismissed. It doesn't matter how independent we Americans want to be of them and their meaning and their demands. There are 12 such words today in the three readings alone, not to mention the other Mass texts. There are 17 such usages gleaned from a quick run-through of the Holy Rule.

Today let's talk playfully—and then seriously—about these concepts. Let's talk about the idea and meaning of dependence, neediness, lack of intelligence, reliance as evident in lamb, sheep and flock and shepherd. Let's do this so as to really discover how lamentable and unnecessary are the difficulties inherent in today's culture regarding these concepts.

To be playful... There's a psychiatric approach that features animals in its method of investigative treatment. "If you were an animal, what animal would you like to be?" the client of the psychiatrist is asked at the first meeting. The question, "If you were an animal, what animal would you like to be?" regularly gets such answers as, "a lion," "a tiger," or "a bird." Now, analysis of such answers leads to therapy, suggesting you can't be a roaring lion and live peacefully. You can't be a growling tiger and live peacefully. You can't fly away like a bird from every annoyance and distress and live peacefully. In-depth analysis says you aren't facing real life in trying. You're desiring to live on controlling as your approach, manipulating as your approach, dominating as your approach. And these approaches meet from other people only greater, unending force from their desire to push their agendas. The therapy then says, "Relax. Try the lamb or the sheep answer. It can work, if you learn to understand it. And when you learn to understand it—it takes long practice—it will work."

Whether you know it or not, I was being playful. Now I'm going to be serious… Monks are people who publicly profess to follow Christ more nearly, and imitate him more closely. Monks are folks who claim Christ as their only teacher, their only lesson, their only sought-after mind transplant, and their only Shepherd. Monks are those who hear Benedict say—and buy into it—"You don't have your own body or your own will under your control. You must walk according to someone else's judgment." Monks are those who ponder Christ—no one else—as the sheep led to the slaughter.

They ponder Christ as the pointed-out Lamb of God. They ponder Christ as the Good Shepherd who knows his sheep, whose job is to lay down his life for them. Monks are real live people, living in a monastery under—that means subject to—an abbot, and under—that means subject to—a Rule. Monks are people who, by profession, desire to be in a flock, with a shepherd guiding them. They seek, they ask, they beg to have an abbot over them, seeing him as necessary to their call. Monks can be the most peaceful people in this vale of tears, and let me tell you, some are. It depends on how seriously they answer by their lives the playful question, "If you were an animal, what animal would you like to be?" In a real sense, this is the continual question in the School of the Lord's Service. "If you were an animal, what animal would you like to be?"

Today, let's let the shepherd here—the abbot (I am he; they already know it)—look at particular members of his flock. Let's let him call them by name. Let's let him remark on their years of taking this approach. Let's be envious of their *Pax Benedictina*, their Benedictine Peace, that they have because of what they are. Let's speak their names—they're getting nervous—let's note their differences, let's be playful and serious. Almost everyone who knows the jubilarians will recognize the playfulness. I pray that the jubilarians on this day of grace will recognize the seriousness.

There's Fr. Marion, who's not here. Fr. Marion is one of six religious, three boys, three girls, all Benedictines. Only one has moved on to God. For years Fr. Marion taught Latin and religion in our high school seminary. Fr. Marion used to take his students down to the lake. He stood on the boat and he taught from the boat... because Jesus did, didn't he? Fr. Marion would take a light bulb—I guess until the procurator got after him for so many—and he would shatter it on the floor saying, "That's what it's like when grace goes." Fr. Marion was the guestmaster for a long time. He took tours through the Abbey Church, and some of the things he said are almost unbelievable. Fr. Marion would say, because the altar was on the cement, "The monks stand on the cement because they have the hard life. The lay people stand on the carpet because they have the easy life." I'd love to hear his explanation now! Fr. Marion is of Monte Cassino fame. For years he was in charge of the pilgrimages. Fr. Marion has many, many friends. Fr. Marion now lives in Tickfaw, Louisiana, and he is a very prayerful person. Fr. Marion is one who says many times, "I'm amazed!" Fr. Marion is always amazed. Fr. Marion is a simple monk; he's a good monk. Fr. Marion is lamb-like.

Then there's Fr. Kevin. Fr. Kevin isn't here. Sixty years, like Fr. Marion, he's in vows. Fr. Kevin is rough, he's ready, he's gentle, he's sweet. At times he's determined, and more frequently he's bull-headed. Fr. Kevin taught physics and math. He was principal of the high school before it closed. Boats, airplanes, motorcycles, ham radios—he loves them all. Fr. Kevin is the tough type. He's a forester. He's now in

Montana. As an old man, Fr. Kevin is still good looking and young looking. Fr. Kevin is prayerful, and he's pious. Sometimes being pious drives us crazy. Fr. Kevin is somewhat lamb-like.

Then we come to Fr. Malachy. He's right here, he's opening his eyes, he's wondering. [Fr. Malachy exclaims aloud: "I'm waiting!"] You can already tell Fr. Malachy is a New Yorker. Fr. Malachy is a gentleman. He's a classic gentleman, according to the New York style of his time. Fr. Malachy is a worker, a hard worker. Fr. Malachy lived 45 years outside the monastery, and he was always a monk outside the monastery. This expression gives meaning to a phrase that we often hear in our necrology when we read about the people who have died and gone on. The phrase goes like this: "He spent much of his monastic life in parish ministry." Fr. Malachy was a monk outside, and he's a monk inside. Fr. Malachy is always the monk. He's obedient, he's willing, he's pleasant, he's jovial, he's tolerant of others. He lives simply. He requires little, and he asks for little. To repeat, and to highlight, Fr. Malachy is obedient, although it is said that he preaches too long. Fr. Malachy is very lamb-like.

Now, Fr. Theodore Brune, we come to you. We call him by his last name because we have another Fr. Theodore [Heck], who is 96 years old, and if he lives until next year, he'll have 75 years of vows. What does one say about Fr. Theodore Brune? Fr. Theodore Brune is different from his brother, Fr. Meinrad, but Fr. Theodore Brune is different from the rest of the world. Fr. Theodore was a Brother for many years, and there are endless stories about those days. He worked in the kitchen, he worked in the sacristy, he was in the guest dining room, he was Abbot Ignatius's valet. One story I remember: He was cleaning the votive light in the Blessed Sacrament Chapel and he fell. He said, "Oh my God!" Somebody said, "Brother!" And he said, "I haven't finished—'help me!'" Fr. Theodore Brune went to Peru as a brother. He went to Rome to the Beda College. He became a priest. If you meet anyone who was at Sant' Anselmo during the time Br. Theodore was there, they tell you that when he preached he said some words in English, some in Italian, some in Spanish—but the gestures carried it all. Fr. Theodore now helps in the Diocese of Fargo, North Dakota. The other day I was talking to an abbot, and he said, "I visited Blue Cloud Abbey, and guess who was there!" Blue Cloud's in South Dakota, but Fr. Theodore was there. Fr. Theodore is irrepressible, he's unpredictable, but he's kind. You meet him and you'll never forget him. Is he for real? Much more so than the askers. What you get is what he is. Is he lamb-like? Well, he's a frolicking one.

Fr. Gavin is a monk. Let me say that again. Fr. Gavin is a monk. He's simple, but he's elegant. He taught speech, and he directed plays for 40 years. Fr. Gavin is regular in his observance; he's very regular. Fr. Gavin is cultured, and yet he's simple. He knows so much about art and architecture and music. But he also knows how to sweep a floor and do it well and willingly. Fr. Gavin has been so good to his friend, Fr. Cyril, in his need. Fr. Gavin loves the monastic life, and he lives it. Fr. Gavin is so respectful of the abbot, and it doesn't matter who the abbot is. Fr. Gavin is a lamb, and he edifies the flock.

Fr. Noah. Do you know that Fr. Noah had the nerve, on the day of my election, to introduce me as "an extrovert's extrovert"?! Fr. Noah wrote the book. Fr. Noah is endlessly talented. He's a singer; you should get him on *Danny Boy*. He's a preacher, a great preacher. He's a spiritual director. People love Fr. Noah, and they rely on him. Fr. Noah loves his family, and he thinks there's only one nationality; read the letters to the editor in *The Criterion*. Fr. Noah knows how to have a good time. Fr. Noah is a tremendous asset to the Archdiocese of Indianapolis. He is stationed outside the monastery, but he's loyal to the monastery, and he's here for every important occasion that he can be. Fr. Noah proudly claims Saint Meinrad. He is just celebrating 25 years, but he's a wise man. Fr. Noah is a lamb, and he's an itchy lamb.

Br. Benjamin. Br. Benjamin can do anything, and he does

it. Br. Benjamin is a fireman, an infirmarian, a plumber, a first-alert man. Br. Benjamin has a marvelous memory; he comes to choir and he sits without a book and he recites and he sings. I watch him; his lips move; I believe that he's saying what we are. It's as if he has a TV monitor inside. In his quiet way, Br. Benjamin does a lot of counseling. He's insightful; he can size up a situation and a person. Br. Benjamin likes to arrive at the last minute. Br. Benjamin is a willing person who knocks himself out to help. He's good to his mother, and he says he's with her a lot. (Sometime I'm going to ask her.) Br. Benjamin is a lamb, but he's a disappearing one. Now you see him, now you don't. Br. Benjamin is somewhere in the flock.

Fr. Harry. Fr. Harry is very learned and Fr. Harry is kind. Fr. Harry is perceptive, forgetful, even a little foggy. Fr. Harry is fun-loving and a true friend to his friends. Fr. Harry is compassionate. He is a student of Sacred Scripture and a student of chant. He created something they call chant fonts, and people on that machine in Fr. Tobias' office are forever asking for his chant fonts. Fr. Harry knows about orchids...and he knows about church renovation. Fr. Harry is a provost turned novice/junior master. Fr. Harry is thoughtful, challenging, and gentle. He's a lamb—if he remembers!

What a proud shepherd I am! You see why? What a great flock we have here. From some of the things I've said today, I could legitimately expect a response like, "Bah, bah." That would be to a few of my words, but not to my thought, really. The happy person, the peaceful person, is not the one who's pushing his or her own will all the time as if it's supreme. The happy person is the one who knows that God's will is supreme. And the happy monk is the one who comes to the monastery to find that out.

Lambs. Sheep. Shepherd. Flock. These are wisdom words. May we never discard them; may we never downplay them. Because if we have Christ, we have peace. And if Christ is our shepherd, there's no life better. I would like to lead a congratulations for these wonderful men. [Applause]

—July 20, 1997,
Profession of Jubilees.
Theology Chapel

PART II

MONASTIC
CONFERENCES

1.

To Change!

My brothers...

My grandmother had an expression, "Half in joke, full in earnest." What I want to say tonight may be a little funny, but I want to make a point. John Pick said, writing of the poetry of Gerard Manley Hopkins, "Unless the man behind the poetry is known, the poetry itself remains obscure." Tonight I want to tell you something about the man behind the poetry.

Cardinal Newman says that when a preacher dies and his sermons are collected, it's discovered he's preached only one theme. We'll begin on the one theme later on. Tonight it's a little bit about the man. One of the reasons I'm telling you a little bit about the man is because it might offer you a bit of reason to understand me. In time I want to know a little more about you, so that I can learn to understand you better.

My home was Pittsburgh, Pennsylvania. I come from a family of eight children: a girl the oldest, a girl the youngest, and six boys in between. I'm the third youngest. My father was Irish descent; my mother was German descent. My father died at the age of 42; I was 13, right when a boy needs his father. (That may explain something.) My father worked for the city of Pittsburgh; he was a politician—an alderman. He worked in the city-county building.

We were poor people; we didn't have much at all. I can remember a couple times at supper I sold my hamburger to my brother, Tom, for a nickel. We didn't have very much at all. We went to a school that was considered the Irish parish,

St. James West End, where twelve grades were together. We were taught by the Mother Seton Sisters of Charity. I was always a favorite of the sisters. In third grade they told me I had a vocation to be a priest, and I believed them. In third grade I was a torch bearer at the altar. (When there were the Solemn High Masses you had the little boys in white cassocks and white surplices and they held the torches. I was one of them.)

The sisters had extreme confidence in me. When I was in eighth grade, Sr. Mary Richard, who taught the third, dropped dead in her classroom. I was summoned to teach third grade. From then on, all the way through until I graduated, when someone didn't show up for class, I was there as the teacher. My sister, Peg, the youngest one in the family, says that she had me in class more than she had anyone else.

In high school, Pittsburgh had just developed what was called the Catholic Forensic League, and on Sundays we did debates, we did extemporaneous speaking, we did memorized declamations, and so many, many, many Sundays in the four years I was involved in speech work. Teddy Maida is a younger brother of Adam, who is the Cardinal now in Detroit. Teddy and I many times were opponents in debates in high school.

When I was in high school, for the last two years I worked at a gas station. We got out of school at 2:55, and I went to work at 3:00, and I did this at least three nights a week and I worked on Saturdays. I didn't know very much about gas stations. The first time I was to change the oil, I let out the antifreeze. I was to check somebody's battery and I stuck my finger in and burnt it. I was told by the boss: "Stay at the pumps." And so I did.

When I graduated from high school—and I graduated the first in class (there were only 35)—I decided that I wanted to study for the Diocese of Pittsburgh. I didn't know anybody else; I didn't know any other priests. I knew the priests at the parish very well because I used to answer the rectory phone sometimes, and I always worked the church bingo.

At this particular time there was a new bishop who came to Pittsburgh whose name was John Dearden. He later on became the Cardinal of Detroit. He had been the rector of the seminary in Cleveland, and a number of seminarians who studied in Cleveland had been at a place called Saint Meinrad. Up until that time Pittsburghers all went to St. Vincent, Latrobe, Pennsylvania. Bishop Dearden decided that all the new students would go to Saint Meinrad. I went to Bishop Dearden and said, "I've never heard of Saint Meinrad and I don't want to go to Saint Meinrad. We're too poor, and it's too far." And Bishop Dearden said to me, "You either go to Saint Meinrad or you don't study for Pittsburgh." So I came to Saint Meinrad.

I was here two years and then I went back to see Bishop Dearden. I said, "Bishop Dearden, now I want to join the monastery at Saint Meinrad." Fr. Gerard had already taken me in to see Abbot Ignatius. And Bishop Dearden said, "Now is the time to study at St. Vincent, Latrobe." So I went to St. Vincent, Latrobe, and I was there for two years, and I went back to see Bishop Dearden and I said, "I want to go to the monastery still." And he said, "I suppose now it's St. Vincent, Latrobe." And I said, "No, it's Saint Meinrad," and he said, "No, you're going to the North American in Rome." And I said, "No, I'm going to Saint Meinrad."

Now I want to tell you what was in my mind at that time. Why did I come to Saint Meinrad? Why didn't I stay at St. Vincent, Latrobe? I liked St. Vincent, Latrobe, very much. One of the Benedictines who stands out in my mind as a model was the great Fr. Quentin Schaut. Fr. Theodore Heck knew him well. He helped to start the American Benedictine Academy. Fr. Demetrius Dumm had just come home from school. He was the prefect on our floor, and ultimately ended up preaching my First Mass. Fr. [now Archbishop] Rembert Weakland had just come home from school, and he was teaching.

But the reason that I chose, so I thought, Saint Meinrad over St. Vincent—and this might be hard for you to understand—was that in my mind at Saint Meinrad no one stood out. Everybody seemed to belong. At St. Vincent, Latrobe, everyone stood out. I thought to myself, "I need to go to a place where I can belong and not stand out." That was why I chose Saint Meinrad over St. Vincent.

Having been in the monastery this long, I'd like to mention the names of three men who especially influenced me, and I'm going to mention people who have died and let the living be free of such acclaim.

The first one who influenced me very much was my novice master, Fr. Bernardine Shine. When I was a novice, I said to him one time, "You needn't think I'm going to come off the mold; I want to be what I am." And Fr. Bernardine said to me, "What you are is what God made you, but what God wants you to become is up as question. You'll have your ideas and I'll have mine, and yours may be more exact than mine, but since I'm in charge you'll go along with me." Fr. Bernardine was someone whom I could talk to, someone who accepted me, someone who really worked hard to try to get me to change a bit.

The next one who influenced me very much was Fr. Abbot Gabriel. When I was newly ordained, I went to St. Benedict's to help where Fr. Gabriel was pastor. Fr. Abbot Gabriel one time said to me as we were riding in the car—I was driving the Volkswagen, he was sitting there with his hands on his stomach, sound asleep—he woke up and he nudged me and said to me, "Do you know why I like you?" And I said, "Fr. Abbot, I can think of thousands of reasons." And he said, "No, do you know why I like you?" And I said, "No." And he said, "Because you say so many things that I think should be said but I'm afraid to say them." Fr. Abbot Gabriel influenced me.

The third one who influenced me—and when you put these three together you'll get some explanation—the third one who influenced me very much was Fr. Alaric Scotcher. Fr. Alaric Scotcher one time said to me, "You could be dropped from a rooftop and you would land on your feet." He had great confidence in me.

When I entered, Fr. Abbot Bonaventure was the abbot. He was elected in June, and we came in July. His was the only abbot's blessing I've been here for. Abbot Bonaventure told me I would do retreat work. I started on retreat work; I hated it. I was scared to death. I came back to him one time and I said, "Fr. Abbot, I have proof positive that I should not be in this work." He asked me what that proof was, and I said, "During this retreat, after each conference, I threw up." And he said to me, "Father, when you give a conference and *they* throw up you'll know you shouldn't be in retreat work."

Thirty-five years have passed, and I probably have given 400 or 500 retreats. I have never liked retreats, I have never asked to give a retreat, and I have never put my shingle out for a retreat. I still go through agony every time I give one. However, I had to work with that, and I've come to the conclusion that it doesn't matter—and I want you to know some of my thinking—whether you like it or you don't like it, as long as you can believe that somehow God wants you to do it. One of the few joys that I think about now in this new position is that I won't be regularly—and I hope not much at all—on the retreat circuit.

We went through the Myers-Briggs here—you may remember that inventory that tells you something about personality—and there were two of us in the community who came out with the same line-up. I think the other one has gone! I'm an ESTJ. Being out with the sisters I've gone through this any number of times, and each time I've ended up an ESTJ. I did the Enneagram—it was forced on me in a couple retreats—and people tell me, because I don't remember, that I'm very much an 8—but an 8 that needs to be redeemed. When we did the conflict management here, I ended up as being high on confrontation and low on avoidance.

But since all of this I have been blessed with cancer... and it's changed my life in many ways. I was really hopeful that the Lord would call me home, but he didn't, at least thus far. I'm not a collector; I pitch. Fr. Abbot Timothy told me, "Do not pitch the two letters you have from Mother Teresa." In the one letter Mother Teresa, after having heard I had cancer, wrote and said, "Jesus is kissing you from the cross." And she asked the question: "Do you want me to ask Jesus to stop kissing you?" And I wrote back and I said, "Mother Teresa, tell Jesus to kiss on, but ask him to make it sweet every once in a while." And the truth of the matter is that the cancer experience has been a sweet experience.

I gave a retreat in New York—Mother Teresa made the retreat—and we had many conversations, and she came to me after several of the conferences and said, "Father, we're so glad to have you. So many priests come in and tell us we're so good and they don't know what they can possibly say. You have come in each time and you have told us to shape up. We appreciate that."

Cardinal Newman says, "To live is to change. To have changed often is to have become perfect." If we're not changing, we're not living; we're just existing. And I have to say that I never thought that I would be elected abbot, but the community has allowed me to change. And I want to do everything that I can to help everyone of you change. So often what we do is we get a picture of each other and freeze that, and 30 years later we're saying, "That's the way a person is." Well, that's not true. We're all changing, and we have to be willing to see this. We have to be willing to accept each other.

I had heard before the election—and you know we did have two years to prepare for election—that I was a possibility. But I really felt that when the dirty wash was done, and I was reviewed, there wouldn't be much chance at all. It didn't work out that way. And so, I was elected, I have accepted, and I will try to be myself.

Up until a few days ago I never set an alarm, except to get up for Midnight Mass at Christmas, cursing the fact that I had to get up. Now I've started to set an alarm, because my sleep pattern's been a little different, and the timing's been a little different. I'm usually up by 4:00, and when I walk out of the cell I'm all ready to go, having wiped up my bathroom floor and made my bed. I like to get to church, I like to pray—I need to pray.

These days have been very interesting days. I really haven't felt especially nervous, and all I can say is somehow you asked for it. I'm going to be as good to you as I can. Because I say what I think, I think it's only fair that you'll say to me what you think. And there is that saying, *Fortiter in re, suaviter in modo*: What we do, let's do forcefully, but let's do sweetly.

We're in a school. It's called the School of the Lord's Service, and I think it's extremely important that we have a steady flow of doctrine. Whether you believe it or not, I don't think I know everything. And so I will be asking other people to give conferences, but conferences we will have. There is a definition that goes: "Education is moving forth from cock-sure ignorance to thoughtful uncertainty." I want to learn, and I want to learn from you, and I hope that you will learn from me.

Everything that I have as far as clothes is concerned is washable, including the black jackets. Casual for me means black shoes, black socks, black pants, and maybe a blue shirt, although somebody did give me some charcoal socks and I have been wearing them.

This is something of what I'm about. I want to hear something about what you're about as we meet. We're in it together. St. Thomas says, *Causus non datur*: There is no such thing as chance. And I do believe, because I've had to do it to keep going over the years, that God gets us wherever he wants us, no matter through whose machinations, ours or anyone else's.

Fr. Donald is doing a coat of arms for me—and he's going to explain it far more eloquently than I. The coat of arms that I suggested, and that he and Br. Herman worked out (Br. Flavian's doing something for the door) will be something like this: Up in one corner is some kind of a light or a star, because evidently they looked it up and that's what Lambert means; in the other corner is sort of a hatchet or an axe—Lambert was a martyr. (Already I have said, "This is Lambert [the star], and this is the community [the axe].") In the next section there are wavy lines, and that is taken from the coat of arms of St. Vincent, Latrobe. In the bottom there are three something or others, I forget, taken from the coat of arms of William Seton, who was the husband of Elizabeth Seton, the foundress of the Mother Seton Sisters of Charity, and it's part of their motto. So it's Lambert who comes from the sisters through St. Vincent...and Lambert who comes here.

Fr. Abbot Bonaventure told me, when I was a novice requesting my new name in the community, to put down "Lambert" first, second, and third or not at all; "you're going to get it." I put it third, and I got it. Now, you can laugh at this and then I'll stop, because I'll prove I can stop. The motto is going to be right from the window of St. Lambert, and it happens to be, "Blessed are the Meek." Maybe you can help me, and I'll try to help you. And to all of this I would now like to say, "Amen," and I invite you to say the same. AMEN.

—*June 12, 1995*

2.

He Came to Make us Great

My brothers...

A number of years ago, Father Urban was chaplain at the Little Sisters of the Poor. It was a custom that on Sunday afternoon the chaplain would give a conference to the old folks, and then have Benediction. On a particular Sunday, Father Urban gave a conference to the old folks, and he explained to them how we all have enemies, and how difficult this is, and how we have to work with our enemies, and how we really prove our love for God by being kind to our enemies. He made his point very forcefully. He had Benediction. And as he was in the sacristy taking off his vestments, a very, very old woman wandered in, and she said to him, "When you finish, I'll meet you in the parlor."

He went to the parlor, and the very old woman assured Fr. Urban that his talk meant absolutely nothing to her. She had no enemies, and she was insistent about that. (She didn't realize she was making one at the very moment.) But after the conversation went on for some time, Father Urban asked her, "How do you know you don't have any enemies?" And she said, "I have outlived them all."

We all have enemies, and our enemies at times are our brothers and our sisters. The Lord knows this; he talks about it. And he gives us some sort of a pattern that we should approach when we know the experience. He says, "If you have something against your brother, go talk to him."

Anytime we try to interpret the Word of God, we have to do it with prudence. St. Thomas Aquinas says that prudence is the right way of doing things. Catherine MacCauley, the foundress of the Sisters of Mercy, says no virtue is perfect without prudence.

When we can foresee that good is going to come from what we do, then we must do it. That's prudence. When we can foresee that good is not going to come from what we do, then we must not do it. That's prudence. When we can't foresee, then we must wait until we can foresee. That's prudence.

We have something against our brother. Our brother has something against us. If it's prudent, we should go to our brother. But when we go to our brother we should realize that if we have something against him, he probably has something against us, and we can't go with the approach wherein we say, "Now look, you're all wrong, and I want to tell you something." We have to go with some kind of humility, expecting to hear not only our own words against our brother, but we have to hear the words of our brother which might bring to us something we should think about.

We go to our brother. We do it prudently. More trouble. The Lord says you may not win him. If we don't win him, then what are we to do? The Lord says we are to call in a witness. How are we going to interpret this? Maybe it means we are to go to somebody who knows both of us. And we say to that somebody, "I have difficulty with my brother; I've gone to him and this is what I've done and this is how it's worked out. What do you think I should do?"

It may be that the witness will say something like this to us: "You know, you come off arrogantly. Your approach isn't always the best. It seems that you didn't do what you could have done." We listen to that witness, and we do what that witness suggests, if we're serious about this. We go then to our brother, following the advice of the witness. The Lord says it may work. It may not. If it works, we have won our brother. If it doesn't work, what are we supposed to do? Are we going to say to that person, "I've done enough; now he can crawl to me when he's ready"?

Well, the Lord says we call in the Church. What does this mean? It may mean we go to the Word of God and we dwell on the Word of God to find if there is something that gives us a new direction. Maybe the Word of God will say, "When you're slapped on this side, there is another." Maybe the Word of God will say, "When this is taken [holding up his scapular], there's more." It may be that we go to somebody whom we think epitomizes the Word of God walking, somebody who seems to get along with everybody, and we tell that somebody who represents the Church, the teaching of the Lord, "This is what my difficulty is. This is what I've done, and it hasn't worked. What do you say?" And it may be that that somebody will tell us, "This type can only be cast out by prayer and fasting." And then we have to wonder if it's worth it. And then we try it, thinking it is. And the Lord says we may win our brother. But we may not.

If we haven't won our brother after these measures, we might think, "It's all over." But the Lord doesn't say that. He brings in a couple thoughts that we have to struggle with, to find their meaning. He now talks about us treating the brother like tax collectors treat people, like pagans treat people.

It seems that he's saying, "If you have done that which you can do according to my approach, and it doesn't work, then maybe you can learn the wisdom of the children of this world." Well, what about tax collectors and what about pagans?

Well, pagans have, as their highest standard of practice, "I'll treat you the way you treat me." It may be what we have to do now is to look and see if this brother, whom we've given every opportunity to, at some time seems to let us know he's ready. And if he shows us he wants to treat us this way in readiness, then we should be ready to accept him.

The tax collectors were people who said hello to everybody. "Hello." "Hello." They said hello to everybody because they wanted to get into the back pocket and get the money. Maybe the Lord is telling us we should never stop talking to people. That we should give everybody, even our brother who distresses us, the common courtesy we would give a dog on the street. Maybe it means we should never give up saying hello. It doesn't mean we say, "Helllooo!" But it does mean that we are polite; and we're always polite.

And it may be that we do this for a long time, and nothing seems to come of it. We can be terribly heroic in our own sight and say, "Look at all that I have done! And it's now impossible." Well, then, we have to remember if it's impossible for us, it's possible with God. And we have to dump it, so to speak, into the lap of God, and that person must become—somehow—constant in our prayer.

If we're offering our gift at the altar, and we have something against somebody, what does the gift mean? Well, right now, after all these steps, it may mean that the person is the gift we offer. And maybe we offer that person in agony. And it just could be that, as long as we live, we never work it out with this person. But if we are praying for this person, it may be that we'll learn somehow, at some time when time isn't, that our prayer for that person was our means of salvation. And maybe we'll learn that our prayer for that person taught us what prayer really means.

We live together; we're brothers. Almighty God has brought us together. He wants us to be together. And if we are people who are following the way of life that we call Benedictine, then we have to do as much as we can to be at peace. Our Holy Father Benedict says, "Don't let the sun go down without having made peace with your brother." The Holy Father says in another place, "If one gets the impression that one of his seniors is angry or disturbed with him in any way, however slightly, he must then and there, without delay, cast himself on the ground at the other's feet to make satisfaction, and lie there until the disturbance is calmed by a blessing."

This is something we can't play with. The Lord asks, "How can you love God whom you do not see if you do not love your brother whom you do see?" And avoidance, and getting up, and walking away when another person comes, simply is not Christian.

And we needn't think that the people who have gone before us had smooth sailing and everyone smiled at them. You've heard of St. Thérèse. Well, she was canonized early. And in the process there were a lot of things that were said in testimony in the early stages. And the people who lived with her spoke of her. A particular Sister who lived with her was named Sister Mary Magdalene of the Blessed Sacrament. And in her testimony she said:

> Sister Thérèse preferred to do good to those from whom she expected neither joy nor comfort nor tenderness. I was one of those. From the time I entered until she died I never felt any natural affection for her. I avoided her. This was not because of any lack of esteem. Quite the contrary. I found her too perfect. If she had been less so, it would have encouraged me. I don't think I was ever a source of comfort to her. Still, she did not desert me, but she showed me a lot of kindness.

You know how we're defined now as religious? It used to be we always talked about all the vows, and that's fine. But we're defined as people who follow Christ more closely and imitate him more nearly. And so tonight I suggest to all of us—if we have something against a brother—prudently, with the help of a confessor, with the help of a director, with the help of a friend, let's do something about it. Because, if we don't, then we're holding ourselves back; and when we hold ourselves back, we hold the community back. We're all in the School of the Lord's Service. Nobody graduates. We have to keep trying. It's hard. But Jesus didn't come to make life easy; he came to make us great. Something to think about, and pray about, for all of us, without exception, starting with me.

—*August 21, 1995*

3.

To Change Often

My brothers...

From 1953 to 1955, I was in school at St. Vincent, Latrobe. Those years were spoken of as "philosophy" years. We had a text which I know a number of you used. It was written in Latin. It was written by Joseph Gredt, the famous Benedictine, who was supposed to be so spacey that if a light bulb burned out, he needed help. He was quite a philosopher. We spoke of his first volume as "Gredt," and the second volume as "Re-Gredt."

I remember Fr. Oliver Grosselin, who was quite a teacher, having been a student of Joseph Gredt, explaining clearly to us the different ways to define. He spoke of the metaphysical, essential definition. This is the definition that speaks of man as a rational animal.

I was always fascinated by what was called the descriptive definition. Man was spoken of as a "featherless biped." The descriptive definition was arrived at *per congeries accidentium*—we had to memorize all of that—*through the bringing together of accidents*, and enough of them so that what is defined is seen to be different from everything else. The accidental definition, or the descriptive definition, sorta puts the parts of the puzzle together.

Tonight, for a specific purpose—and you'll see it as time goes on—I would like to tell you something about my thought pattern, which, of course, is established by my background and my make-up and my experience, and by special influences in my life. And in so doing I think I will be approaching some sort of an inadequate, but yet a descriptive definition of me.

I've said before that in my monastic life, according to my thinking, I have especially been influenced by three people: Fr. Bernardine, my novice master; Abbot Gabriel, whom I helped as a young monk when he was at St. Benedict's; and Fr. Alaric. And so my definition is somehow tied to what I accepted from them and from other people, and from the experiences of life, and then what I rejected from what experience and people brought me.

I'd like to go now by examples.

- I like people to be where they're supposed to be. I like monks at choir time to be in choir.
- I like monks to be on time. For everything.
- I think that fellow monks should not just do things for us, but also, and especially, be with us.
- I don't think monks should keep any monies without permission, or spend any monies without permission.
- I'm convinced that if monks don't pray their Office regularly as obligation, they won't be able to see any obligation for choir attendance. If they don't have to do it, why should they do it, when it can be a drag or a pain, according to their thought?
- Originally—and I use this word to show that thoughts can change—I didn't want anything beyond adequate heating, air conditioning, choir stalls, a good sound system, and a few more repairs to make up the church renovation.
- I don't think that monks should go beyond their assigned destination when they're out, unless the superior knows this beforehand, or is told it afterwards.
- It seems to me that monks should not have use of cars or trucks as if they were their own, for their

personal comings and goings.

- I'm against what I could call—because I've heard it so spoken of—little kingdoms within the monastery.
- I think some few monks do not take my requests for silence and whispering seriously enough.
- I think some monks show lack of common courtesy by their apparent coldness and indifference to their brethren, not even greeting and welcoming those returning after long absences.
- It seems to me that monks should wash themselves and their clothes frequently, and not reek of body odor to the discomfort of their brethren.
- I am of the opinion that people should speak their minds in the right place, to the right people, and in the right way, and not constantly murmur behind the scenes, establishing such an approach as a way of life for themselves.
- I don't approve of monks not speaking to each other.
- It seems wrong to me for monks to refuse to sit next to any certain person in choir.
- I think at meals, when we can choose where to sit, that we ought to circulate, at least betimes.
- Traveling to many gatherings of Benedictine men and women, like those recently at the Congress at Monte Cassino and Subiaco, I find that everyone attending is invited to choir for the occasion or meeting. I approve of this. The approaches that I'm taking I take to prayer. And I try to balance these approaches against our traditions, the signs of the times; and I move with advice, often asking people who may be more objective than I.
- I believe people can change. I really believe especially in the vow of *conversatio*. One of the reasons I believe in it is that I think I have changed, and changed a lot. And I know that I have a lot to go. But because I believe that people can change—and I

know that they should change—I try to give people chances for change, over and over again. There isn't any monk I have a frozen picture of. There isn't any monk I have given up on. If it happens that I'm taken advantage of because of this approach, I ask the question: Whose fault will that be? Then I also say, knowing myself: How long will I tolerate it?

- I think it's okay for people not to volunteer on principle, but I think those people should tell the superior this, so he can assign them as need arises.

I guess I'm saying that I'm a featherless biped; I'm a human being; I'm a rational animal. And I think that the accidental definition approach fits for me, and helps gradually to put the pieces of the puzzle together for you.

Now all of you—and each one of you—have your ideas, your thought pattern, and this comes from your background, your make-up and your experience, along with the special influences of people in your life. You, as I, move with what you choose to accept, and what you choose to reject. So we all have the same challenges from life, even though we necessarily approach them differently because we're different.

In time—and I think this is terribly important—we should learn that we can't live with life as we think it should be; we have to learn to live with life as it is. And so, because I don't always have my way, and you don't always have your way—and we're not always supposed to have our way—I suggest a few directives for all of us.

- I suggest that we accept the fact that we don't all think alike. And I think somehow we can say that's okay. I think that we should not demonize those who take different views or approaches from ours. I don't think we should be tied with the thought that people are bad guys because their minds work differently, or they're at a different stage in spirituality.

- I think that we all need to learn when to speak and when to keep quiet. I especially think that we need to recognize that any anger that abides in us may easily be our own fault...because we always want our way, and we're mad if we don't get it.

- I think that we'd better be careful not to try to hold the community captive by pushing our views in improper ways. When we don't like something, there's an outburst. When we don't like something, there's a shouting match. When we don't like something, there's inappropriate language. I don't think anyone of us, as a member of this community, should be held captive to anybody who takes this approach with regularity. And I think anyone who takes this approach at an individual time should be told about it, and told directly.

- I'm convinced that the most disliked people in the community are those who have to have the last word, those whose approach to life is the "this or nothing" method, those who always correct and always distinguish, and are forever putting the record straight. I think the most disliked people in the community are those who spend endless time saying it as they see it, while equating it with the way it is.

- I think that all of us need the Gospel as our guide, and I think the Gospel has a lot to say about what I'm emoting over tonight. You know, it would be interesting to see how many times in the Rule we hear an expression like this: "Let the abbot decide." "Let the abbot hear everyone and then decide." "Let the abbot arrange." It so happens that maybe not you, but this community, elected me; and I'm the abbot. And I think when you have your view, and you hear mine, you ought to weigh mine a little bit.

This is not meant to be a tirade. I'm not mad at anybody. I'm not bawling anybody out. If I were doing that I would be a little more lively. But what I am saying is that there are a number of things I think we should look at. There should be a lot that we dislike about ourselves—in a very healthy manner. Because if we do, we might just be moved to do something about ourselves. And if we do, maybe almost everybody we live with will benefit from it.

We can change our views. Sometimes we do. Maybe we're in a frame of mind on a particular situation where we can't change our views. If we can't, we certainly can change the manner of expressing them, if the manner is a bit out of order.

We're going to stop soon and we're going to pray Compline. In the Compline book it talks about coming for a moment to an examination of conscience before we actually enter into the prayer. So I would say that if there's something that I've said tonight to you, having talked out loud to myself, maybe there is need for a moment of examination—and maybe there will be a moment before we start the prayer. Amen.

—January 13, 1996

4.

I Ask A Lot of You

My brothers...

Tonight I'd like to touch upon several subjects, and this won't be a conference as such, at least on a particular topic.

A number of people ask me from time to time, "How is your health?" So I want to tell you a little bit about my health. I seem to be doing very well. Recently I had a blood exam, and only in two areas was I a little bit off. The rest of it was fine. My cholesterol is 173. The little bit that was off, so Br. Daniel tells me, can be taken care of by a bit of exercise. I used to do a good bit of walking, and I haven't done too much recently. So I have started to walk again, coming to the church a little earlier than the early coming, and I'm walking there, and I think it's helping me. I feel good. I have varicose veins in the left leg, and when I preach four or five times, I have to put that leg up for a while and rest.

The doctor told me the last time that I should get lots of rest and stay away from stress. [Much laughter.] I try to get away from stress, and I try to take a little rest. My blood pressure's a bit high. I guess a lot of people's blood pressure is high. Once you have the colon operated on and they take 18 inches of it out, things don't work the way they did before. And one can stay on a particular diet and be very careful, but I choose to eat what I want, and then take the consequences. And every so often there are consequences. Along with the blood pressure pill that I take, I now take a diuretic, so I can be running for different reasons.

My health is good. Thank you for asking.

I think that the spirit of silence is improving. When I say, "Whisper," I don't mean, "Wherever you are, always talk quietly." I mean: if you must talk or you have something to say, it's good to be quiet so that we don't disturb other people who may be more recollected than we are. I especially appreciate the fact that, in the morning when we go to breakfast, it's quiet in there. People who have to say hello to each other—and people are different—seem to be saying hello a little more quietly.

I'd like to say what we hear frequently—and I don't know how true it is—80% of the work is done by 20% of the people. But when we ask for volunteers, it would be good if people would volunteer who don't usually volunteer. Some people volunteer all the time, and there are some who volunteer all the time who perhaps shouldn't—because then they become martyrs, and they may do the work, but their attitude isn't just the best.

We shouldn't volunteer just when it's convenient. We certainly should volunteer when it is convenient. But when it's a little inconvenient, then it shows something about us, and tells us something about our makeup, and tells other people something about our makeup. The Gospel doesn't say, "Shine your light," but it does say "Let your light shine." And very often when there is need, we see light shining, because people are willing to move in and help.

I'd like to remind all of us that, because of the upcoming building program, there's going to be a need for a lot of patience. We're going to have to figure out where we will be worshipping, and where we will be doing a number of things. And so, I think we should prepare for all of this. And we should be conscious of the fact that things won't go for any of us the way we want them to.

You know, we can learn a little bit about this from people who live outside, people in families, who have children to take care of, who have jobs to drive to, who are constantly involved in traffic, who have all kinds of unexpected things coming up. I think for us as monks, we are given the great blessing of a schedule, and then we get very disturbed if the schedule doesn't go our way.

I remember reading something from Henri Nouwen, wherein he said, "When I was young I resented interruptions in my schedule. And now that I'm older I have learned that interruptions are my schedule." It just doesn't go the way any of us wants it to. We certainly are entitled to make suggestions as to where we will be and what we will do when the renovation takes place, but then we have to accept the end conclusions.

We did give out, through a committee, the chance to talk about recreation. And some suggestions have come in. We have put those suggestions and the numbers that answered the questions on the board. And there are some people who would like to play cards. There's a great number that would like to play cards. I say to those who would like to play cards now: Do something about playing cards. Talk to the people who gave out the questionnaire. Maybe we'll put a sign up then: *Who Wants to Play Cards Tonight?*

You know, we are great with the ideas, and sometimes we're not much with the follow-through. We had a Father in our community, some of you may remember him. His name was Fr. Urban. And there was a German quote that he used to use frequently: *"Gross im Kopf, Klein im Sack"* (Big in the head, and little in the pocketbook). In other words, there's not too much follow-through. Fr. Urban also used to say, "It looks good on paper."

I was very touched last week with the retreat that Fr. Adelbert gave. It was a fine retreat. But I was more touched by the fact that one of our own did it. And it went well. And we accepted him. And Fr. Adelbert was personally very, very pleased. He's travelled the globe. He's given retreats everywhere.

You know, it's all right to somehow change what is a passage in Scripture. A prophet can be received in his own hometown. We all have lots to give. We all do. And we have talents that we don't really know we have. Very often our talents are only tapped if we're given something that is beyond that which we thought we would ever do. The truth of the matter is that we do have some talents that fit very well with us emotionally, and then there are other talents that don't. And so, in exercising some talents, we have to have a little bit of suffering.

We have this gathering now of abbots and presidents of federations and superiors and a Cistercian abbess here. And we're hearing a number of talks on leadership. Fr. Eugene is giving the talks. They're very well done. The commentary that goes on at the tables afterwards is very enlightening. We're no different here than they are there. The specificity now and then may be, but we're all pretty much alike.

And when they come here, they find us so kind and gentle and welcoming—and we are. But I think that it's good if we move this way a little more in reference to each other. It's hard to be kind to the people we live with all the time. And I think a very practical way of being kind toward each other is acknowledging each other. Fr. Eugene's giving those talks. They're good talks. If I hear that, I should say, "Fr. Eugene, you're giving good talks."

It seems, in a way, that "thank you" can be a phrase

that's missing. It may be that some have the idea that, if they say thank you, or they congratulate, they're somehow taking something away from themselves. That's not true. They're just showing that there are people beyond themselves, and there is a bit of heart that goes out to those people.

They tell me that I should take a day off once in a while. You might think, well, you're gone. It's a little different. I was gone over the weekend. It was very interesting, preaching four times. Some preached more than four times. There are some who don't get out much who have the idea that, if somebody's out, automatically it's rah-rah. Well, it isn't automatically. Once in a while it is rah-rah. And some of the ones who don't get out all that much, get out every so often, and they get out specifically for rah-rah. And that's all right.

We understand very well what we do. We understand people who think like we think. We understand the faults we have. But the others … We can look to that a little bit.

I remember one time someone saying, "One thing about me, I'm not jealous." But it could have been that the person was so proud there'd be no reason for him to be jealous of anyone. It doesn't necessarily mean that if we don't have a particular vice, we automatically have a virtue. No.

It's a little over seven months since that day [of my election as abbot]. And I must say that you people have been very supportive and kind to me. And I appreciate it. Only one or the other jutted his chin a little bit at me, and usually, when that happens, it's in my makeup to jut a little more. It isn't the office that brings the jut; it's the makeup.

I'm willing to talk to anybody about anything, and I'm surprisingly calm. There must be the grace of office. And I want to be for you a good abbot. And that's why twice a day

I pray this prayer that I gave you right after the election. And I'm going to stop now. But before I stop, I want to pray this prayer out loud. It will be my second time today. And I want you to hear once more what this prayer says. There are some days when it's hard to pray it, because it asks a lot. I ask a lot of you. You have a right to ask a lot of me. And the only way you can give, and I can give, is if we pray. And so now I pray:

> You know my heart, Lord, and that, whatever
> you have given to your servant, I desire to
> spend it wholly on them, and to consume it all
> in their service.
>
> Grant to me then, O Lord my God, that your
> eyes may be opened upon them day and night.
>
> Tenderly spread your wings to protect them.
> Stretch forth your holy right hand to bless them.
> Pour into their hearts your Holy Spirit who may
> abide with them
> while they pray
>
> to refresh them with devout compunction,
> to stimulate them with hope,
> to make them humble with fear,
> and to inflame them with charity.

May He, the kind Consoler, sustain them in temptation, and help their weakness in all the trials and tribulations of this life. Amen.

—*January 15, 1996*

5.

I Am A Monk

[Father Abbot reads Chapter 49 of the Holy Rule.]

My brothers...

A number of years ago, our Fr. Vincent was visiting at Prince of Peace, at the time called St. Charles. There was a rather famous monk there. He had come from Sienna in Italy, and he joined the monastery of St. Andrew in Belgium. He founded a mission in China, was imprisoned, was expelled, and he went back to Belgium, and then finally came to the United States where he founded the monastery at Valyermo. His name was Fr. Raphael Vinciarelli, and he was a marvelous man.

Fr. Vincent met him at St. Charles, and he asked him, "Fr. Raphael, what do you do?" And Fr. Raphael said, "I am a monk." And Fr. Vincent said, "You don't understand me. (Fr. Vincent is great for clarification.) What do you do?" And Fr. Raphael said, "I am a monk."

Monks do some things, some that are so important that they somewhat identify what a monk is. We hear many kinds of "oughts." Some people say everybody ought to see the Grand Canyon, and see God's grandeur. Some people say every monk of Saint Meinrad ought to see Einsiedeln. Those are interesting oughts, but they're not moral imperatives.

There are things that monks ought to do that are moral imperatives. Every *ought* that is really an obligation can be traced back ultimately to *synderesis*—good must be done, evil must be avoided. And there are certain things that monks, to be monks, ought to do. In the passage from the Holy Rule we just read, our Holy Father says the life of a monk ought to be a continuous Lent. But he says few have strength enough for this. But when the real Lent comes, monks ought to be monks. And they ought to do what they ought to be doing, so that when the season is over they can carry to their life that which maybe before they haven't done, and ought to do, and have done now for forty days, and now can do, because practice is established.

What are some of the "oughts" that monks ought to do, and don't always have the strength for, but have the holy season upon them, offering its grace? I think that in the last few months when we've been together in this situation, there's been some spelling out of what we ought to do. If we are religious, we ought to center our lives in the celebration of the Eucharist. If we are Benedictines, we ought to be very careful to prefer nothing to the Work of God. If we are followers of St. Benedict, and we are to live in community, and we are to correct each other, and grow through this correction, then we ought to go to our brother when we have something against him and tell him, instead of telling everybody else, or instead of coming immediately to the abbot to report.

We ought to be more silent. In our own little way around here, we've been saying we ought to whisper. Some don't like to whisper. Some are hard of hearing. Some don't agree with whispering. Some think they should talk whenever they want to talk. But do these things somehow fit with the ought?

You know, the season is at hand. We're told in the Holy Rule that during Lent we ought to read a book all the way through. We ought to. I would suggest that we all read a book, all the way through. I'm not saying the Holy Rule, though. I'm saying we ought to read the abbot's conferences that are available in the reading room. They spell out some of the oughts that we've already talked about, and have somewhat established, so they can come back to our minds and move into our practice.

We ought to be where we ought to be, when the time tells us to come. This is a communal something. If we would all take this seriously, then when the joy of Easter comes, the joy would be magnified. We live together; we owe a lot to each other. The choir is not for a few. It's not for the compulsives; it's not for those who find it convenient; it's not for those who like the pace. It's for everyone. I've said this before, and I repeat it: Since I've been abbot, there are two people who have asked to be excused from choir. We know that everybody can't be at choir, but we know—and we can pick this up if we read that little book, those papers, those talks—that if we can't be in choir, we ought to pray the Office that we have missed. If we don't, we're saying to ourselves and each other that it's not important and why should we come anyhow.

These 40 days can be very good days. The reason the *Bona Opera* wasn't passed out before is that I'm hoping that, from a few of the things that are said tonight, we can put something down on the paper and pay attention to it. Not extra things. Not the things we'll drop. But the things that we can move into because we ought to, so that practice is ours, and virtue is learned.

Over and above all of this that we all ought to do, we come to the individuality of each one of us. And we are individuals. And we ought to look at what we can do individually, and should do individually, because we're not doing individually what we should be doing individually. The eighth degree says the monk does only what is endorsed by the common rule of the monastery and the example set by the seniors.

You know how people drive us crazy by those eccentricities they have. We can point them out readily; we can talk about them readily. And they should do something about those eccentricities. But so many of us seemingly don't know our own. We don't know how we get on each other's nerves because we don't do what is the common practice. If I would start with examples tonight—I could give many of them—I would be somehow identifying some people, and pointing them out as peculiar. That's not enough. We're all peculiar in some of the ways we go on our own.

And so it would be nice if we would look to ourselves and see what we do that we know disturbs other people, or is so much different from what the community does. It's not big things that disturb. It's the little things. And it may be, because this is something that ought to be developed, that we could go to a particular person and say, "You do this; this bothers. You're probably not conscious of... Why don't you consider...?" We should be correcting each other. We're all here for the same purpose: to move into the fullness of life, and to become saints. Reward is given to each. We don't seem to have developed that too well. That has to be done humbly and simply. And it requires that the person who hears it—and any one of us can hear it—is ready to hear it. Because the person wants to get better, and hearing what he ought to do, he's willing for it.

But we know how human nature is. And a lot of those other people won't really accept it. Would we accept it? Do we accept it? A correction, a suggestion? Well, since it's so terribly hard to suggest and to find within self, in the Holy Rule, in chapter 72, we read: "We should support one another with the greatest patience." And what do we support? We support the weakness of the other, whether that weakness be of body or behavior.

And so, it's a good time. It's a serious time. It's a time of great hope. Let's not take on the extras, please, unless we have fulfilled already in our lives what we're talking about. But let's pray together. Let's come to the Eucharist together. And if for any reason we can't, let's make sure that we are silently praying and joining in with the community.

There is some place in the Rule where an ought is laid on the abbot. He ought to visit the cells of the monks. And so, during Lent, the abbot will visit the cells of the monks. There will be a sign put up, explaining when. It will be in and out. Those cells that are listed can find their residents standing at the door at the designated time.

We want to move together. We have a lot of things to face, you know that. Tomorrow we have to face a new schedule. Pretty soon we'll face the renovation of the church. We'll face worshipping in a new place. And those are important things, and we have to be ready for them. But what's all important is the reason for which we came. And that is to become saints. And this [showing the Rule] is a proven way of life, and it's all in here. And, specifically, we're now talking about this season.

We all take turns with our psychological problems. We all try to work them out. Sometimes we do them with psychiatrists or counselors. But one of the things that we should remember is this: We will never be able to work them out unless we work them out within the context of the common life. We don't work our problems out by writing our own schedules, and having our own plans, and going our own way. We work them out within the context of the monastery. And so, I say, the season is here.

I'm going to say this. Maybe I'll find out if I'm strong enough really to say it. I would welcome suggestions from you as to what I ought to do, so that I can change. I need you, and you need me. It's just the way the life goes. And so I say please, please, please, in these 40 days, let's live as we ought to be living. And if so... my, my, it can be great for each and every one of us. Amen.

—February 20, 1996

6.

ANGER—
AND FORGIVENESS

My brothers...

I have been fascinated by the visitation report, both the public one and the one for the abbot alone. Already, in various ways, I have dealt with the suggestion of fraternal correction with the talk about expressing our own minds. I've dwelt now and then on confrontation. Tonight I would like to read two selections from the recessus report, and then comment on them. The one is entitled "Care of the Sick":

> We are impressed with the care you provide for the physically ill and the aged in the infirmary under the able guidance of Br. Daniel. You do manifest fidelity to chapter 36 of the Holy Rule, that care of the sick must rank above and before all else, so that they may truly be served as Christ. You seem to grasp the unique importance of the sick for providing a special opportunity to witness an important monastic value.

> We think that you could work harder at extending such a faith vision to other members of the community who, although they may not be physically ill, do manifest signs of suffering from various forms of psychological and spiritual illness. Christ is also to be found in those

who, over the years, have developed a certain
mental imbalance, have become hurt or alienat-
ed, who in many ways tax us with excessive
demands on our charity. A community must not
fail in its charity toward all.

The second quote:

You need to admit and deal with hurt and anger
in your relations. Emotions that sometimes go
far back in a given monk's history, and have in
effect made him in a certain way sick, if not
dysfunctional.

Let's talk about all of this tonight in a generic way as
anger, deep-seated anger within members of the community.
Anger is something that's common; it's experienced every-
where. It's common enough for monks. When I was at the
meeting of the abbots at St. Joe's, Louisiana, I talked to a
monk who said his entire community was so filled with
anger that the community was undergoing group therapy,
and each individual member was dealing with a psychologist
or psychiatrist.

The angry person holds himself captive, and sometimes
holds the community captive. And sometimes for years on
end.

Anger often serves as the main principle from which
one's thinking and acting proceeds. Anger can be because of
big things, or little things, but they're things that preoccupy
the mind and the heart of the individual involved. Anger can
be somewhat rational, or totally irrational. The reason for
anger is often blamed on other people, or it fixates itself on
one person in particular. This anger fixation is often enough
fixed on authority figures—a particular one, or anyone who
happens to occupy the chair.

This anger may come from disappointments; it may
come from jealousy. It may come from resentment. It may

come from not getting what one wants or from not being con-
sulted in one's expertise. It may come from being passed over
or not being heard. It may come from never being praised or
appreciated. It comes, for sure, from life not working out as it
should, that is, as the individual wants it to.

Anger almost always appears to the individual as legitimate. And for some it even appears to be virtuous. There is
the passage in Scripture that says, "Be angry and sin not."
But that's not anger across the board. When cultivated as a
right, or suffered as an ailment, or experienced in combina-
tion, anger may require the help of a psychologist or a psychiatrist. It may need therapy; it often demands medical help.
Sometimes it goes into hospitalization. But, inevitably, it
requires a new way of thinking if change is ever to be in
store.

It requires thinking based on seeing life differently,
and—specifically for the monk, this means seeing life differently in the monastery. One has to learn not to be bound, tied
up by anger. And one has to learn not to bind others by it.

Anger, when it is good, is anger which is on a leash.
And it knows how to express itself appropriately. Anger
which is out of line shows itself in open and hidden ways.
Through meanness. Through undue self-protectiveness.
Through the disappearing act: getting off the scene. Through
passive aggression. Through excessive demands. Through
endless pushing for one's rights. Through criticism. Through
clever remarks. Through put-downs. Through arrogance.
Through eccentricity which is cultivated eccentricity. Through
rejecting the schedule. Through not turning in money.
Through coming late to everything. Through not coming
when one doesn't want to. Through murmuring.

Anger's displays are endless. And its consequences for
community can be devastating: not speaking to others; getting up and moving when someone comes into the room;
refusing to sit at the same table with others; rudeness; open
rejection; avoidance. All this helps to make others feel worth-
less, uncomfortable, unwelcome, nervous, marginalized, use-

less, or maybe even superfluous.

What to do about anger? How to deal with it? One has to learn to react differently. And this only comes about if one learns to think differently. We can't change our acting until we change our thinking. This means we should work on our anger every day. We should work on it in what we call our examen. Where am I today? What am I doing to help myself today? How much under control am I today?

Help comes through specific prayer: Help me to face the reality. Help comes through confession. Help comes through confrontation, when it's managed well. Such help moves us to move on from this torture and this torturing approach.

What I really want to dwell on tonight in talking about help, and where we can get it, stems from my statement now that we should look at the elements of the Gospel Christ, not according to our frozen image of him which we're comfortable with. But we should look at the Gospel image of Christ, and we should expect to learn rough things that come our way from him. We should learn to expect rejection. We should somehow, in some way, be able to welcome persecution. We should look at non-acceptance as somehow a gift; at suffering as an experience that makes us Christ-like; at mistreatment as that which Christ promises.

Christ doesn't come to make life easy; Christ comes to make us great. Where are those passages in the Gospel that say, "If you are my disciple, take up your cross daily." It doesn't say pick your cross; it says take it. What about the passage that says, "Count it sheer joy when you know suffering." What about the passage that says, "Blessed are you when they persecute you." What about the passage that says, "What can separate us from the love of Christ?" and then gives us the long list?

Cardinal Newman says it is nothing but the cross of Christ, without and within us, which changes any one of us from being a devil into an angel. Look at the Rule of our Holy Father. He says to put up with; don't be constantly complaining and griping about.

You know, we can run off to our cells; we can get away from each other. We're so far removed from what people in their homes have to put up with day after day and night after night. What does St. Benedict mean when he says consider oneself meaner and viler? I mean, is that all jazz? Are there sections like these in the Rule that should be excised, like we would like to cut out some of the prescriptions about arranging the psalms? Doesn't St. Benedict say something about walking according to someone else's judgment: *ambulantes secundum judicium alienum?* Doesn't he say to do what's for the benefit of others and not for ourselves?

If we look at the lives of holy people, people who have proven that they knew what it was all about—because they're over there now in the right place—what did they experience? Were they grouches and complainers, because things didn't go as they thought they should?

You know that man whose name is Alphonsus Ligouri. He got booted from his own home because he was going to be a priest, and his father didn't want him to. He died exiled from the community that he founded. What about Gerard Majella? He was in prison because he was falsely accused of having fathered a child he had nothing to do with. I mean, isn't that element in our lives? Somehow it should be. Hear the words of the some of the sages. Cardinal Newman says it's wonderful to suffer for the Church, but it's magnanimous to suffer at the hands of the Church. Don't we want that which is magnanimous?

I am sure there are some members of our community who thought that certain problems would disappear with a new abbot. Recently I told the former abbot that no doubt some of the same individuals who caused him problems cause me problems—except for the fact that I have one less problem than he did, because I don't have me.

You know, I begged several times in my life, practically on bended knee, to stay in the monastery. And Father Timothy told me it would be better for the monastery if I weren't here. And, you know, he was right. Because I learned

outside the monastery what I couldn't learn here at that particular time. I have no anger toward Father Timothy. I could
say he treated me a bit rough, but I'd have to say, at the same
time, so did I treat him that way. You know, it isn't the one
who wears the [abbot's] cross who necessarily has all the
power. He certainly has all the cross, in a certain sense.

What we need to do is to get some real religion, and not
soupy stuff. If I don't feel like getting up, I don't get up. If I
don't sleep well, I don't get up. If I don't want to go to table, I
don't go to table. If I want to go out, I go out. If I want to
hold back money, I hold back money. What kind of life is
that? We have to get off protecting ourselves, and we have to
get down to laying our lives down. You know, religious are
spoken of as those who follow Christ more closely, and imitate him more nearly.

And so, if you're not getting my point, I'll summarize
the way I see it. We can move from anger if we move to
acceptance. If we move to abandonment. If we move to surrender. If we move to the thought that God might know that
what we're experiencing is going to help us. If we move to
joy. Our friend Abbot Marmion says that joy is the echo of
God's life in us. When the only echo is our own life, there's
no joy. There's constant complaint. We shouldn't be constantly condemning the supposed cause of our anger. We should
condemn somehow in ourselves the real cause of our anger,
and that's our makeup. All anyone else can be is an occasion.

We should ask ourselves somehow: Why am I not holy
enough to deal with this better? We have a proven way of
life, and if we move more and more into it, away from the
manipulation of it, then we'll move from anger. And we'll
move to the best life that we can have in this vale of tears.
Help for all of us, the best help, comes from the life that
we've vowed. Because it brings us more and more into
authenticity.

The people whom I admire very much—and some of
them are right here—are the recovering alcoholics, who face
in the 12 Steps the idea of anger over and over again. I have

experienced outbursts of several people. Those same people, after going to whichever step it is, have come back and said I'm sorry, and have been able to recognize what we who have perhaps thrown our particular examen away are not able to.

It's said that, when there's difficulty, the atheist is asking, Why, why? The believer is asking, What do you want me to learn from this difficulty?

You know, there's that story that's told of Catherine of Siena, and both elements are somehow in our life. She came into the presence of the Holy Father and she spoke of him as my sweet Jesus Christ. And she said the stench of the devil is in the room.

We can find the Lord in any circumstances—if it's the Lord we're looking for, and not ourselves. Leon Bloy said, as an old man, "I'm convinced that that which is always supernatural, or can be, in the world, is suffering."

I know for myself—and I have a long way to go—that I'm much better now because I've been mistreated, because I have met all kinds of difficulty, and because I have somehow had to say, "Lord, have it your way." If I weren't able to say that, somehow, I couldn't be sitting here. And so, what I offer to you is what I try myself.

We have a wonderful community; we really do. I've been to many monasteries and to many communities, as you know. And there's no place that I would rather be on the face of the earth. But we're here to become holy, and if we don't, we're not succeeding.

My novice master (there was an Italian Sister who got things mixed up who used to say my novice "mister") used to say over and over again—and it's that which I'll end with—"There's only one success that God acknowledges. One. And that is holiness." And that success comes from learning how to deal with the Cross, and to know resurrection in and through every experience of it. Amen.

—*April 29, 1996*

7.

TO LIVE IS TO ANNOY

My brothers...

To live is to annoy. To live is to be annoyed. It's part and parcel both ways. We annoy and we are annoyed, because no one is exactly like we are. The Scripture says *non est inventus similis illi*—there's not found one like unto him. And when we say about a particular person, "When God made him, he threw the mold away," we need to recognize that it's true of every single one of us.

Tonight we want to look at annoying and being annoyed. Tonight I want to tell you a little bit about my background, and you can rehearse yours. A lot that's in me comes from my mother; a little bit comes from my father—he died too early. A lot comes from the Mother Seton Sisters of Charity, who taught me for twelve years. A lot comes from Fr. Thomas Brown, who was my pastor for many years, and for whom I worked the bingo. Long before there was such a thing as face-to-face confession, I could go into his confessional, confess my sins, and then he would pull the curtain aside and say, "Bill, come over to the house and take my pants to the cleaners."

I was very much influenced by my novice master, Fr. Bernardine. I was very much influenced by my experience in Calcutta, where people have nothing, and they die on the streets. I have been very much interested in Cardinal Newman over the years, and I think I've been influenced by him.

Let me tell you about some of the characteristics in my

make-up because of this experience. And you can figure out what I have done with these characteristics—whether I, as it were, insist on them in other people, or whether I've learned to be a bit tolerant and understanding when they don't have the characteristics which I'm going to talk about. These will be strange. It's all right; we're all strange.

I was taught never to blow your nose in public. I was taught you don't sit on a desk or a table. I can tell you about sitting on a desk—rather, a table—when I was in third year high school. It was in the chemistry lab. Sister Marie Anthony—and remember, this was in 1949 or 1950—said to me, "Bill, tables were made for glasses, not for ___ ... people to sit on."

We were taught not to cross our legs in church. I remember the first time I saw Fr. Blaise cross his legs. Oh, my goodness, how that moved me some way. My grandmother always said, "Don't yawn in public. If you do, cover your mouth." If I wouldn't, she'd say, "You're going to swallow us all."

My make-up is—and I think I may get some of this from St. Teresa of Avila—if the illness is serious enough, it will declare itself. If I have a headache, I'll have a headache wherever I am, so I'll try to be wherever I'm supposed to be, no matter what the headache is like.

With Cardinal Newman I think I believe that the unseen world is the real world. So I'm very interested in the unseen world. We had a meeting one morning, and there was some mention made of death, and a monk rose to the occasion and said, "Well, Fr. Abbot, not everyone has the view on death that you do."

As far as secrecy is concerned, I think secrecy is marvelous when it has to be, and I think it's lethal when it's used and shouldn't be. I learned to speak directly and to take the consequences. I've had people say things to me that haven't been very nice. At least I thought so. I remember a number of years ago somebody said to me, "You're a complete jackass." And I said to the person, "And you're perceptive." I'm not too much moved by people's strong opinions that way. I'm not too indirect. I meet people, even members of the community, who won't say things to me directly, but they'll say them so that I can hear them. Recently, somebody in the reading room was reading what was in the abbot's column of the *Community Bulletin*, and somebody came to me and said, "I think he's making fun of your approach." And I said, "Until he tells me, I'll pay no attention to it."

For the longest time I've been disturbed because in my bedroom was a phone where you can see the name of the caller on the top of it, and there was a private line, and I had three possibilities of pushing. I didn't want that telephone, nor did I want that private line; I felt it was exorbitant. One of the monks said to me, not knowing how I felt about this, "We want to get one of those phones for our office." And I said, "You can have mine. I'll be thrilled."

One of my friends in the community used to say to me, "You would keep a clinic of psychiatrists busy." I think this is true of all of us. From where we are, and what we're made like, we establish so many principles. And God pity the people who don't, as it were, live according to those principles.

St. Benedict says that in the morning the monk might come late to choir because he's sleepy. I had always been taught to be ahead of time. Never come at the last moment. I had been taught in the novitiate to always come. I don't know—don't remember, and I'm using the word "remember" rather than "recall"—I don't remember ever having to say *culpa* for missing Office. But St. Benedict says that people will be sleepy; give them time. But then St. Benedict says elsewhere that when the bell rings people should leave their work, and with hands disengaged, they should go. I guess this is at a time when St. Benedict presumed people were awake. It's funny, if we were taught to always be on time, we could think that those who aren't on time are somehow at fault, couldn't we? It's all mixed up there some way.

When we come to the monastery, and we come with all these different backgrounds, we need something to direct us and to straighten us all out, so that we can learn to give and take. And, I think, what can help us along these lines is what we consider the customs of the house, the things that have been handed down, the way we do things as a community. And then I think we can all buy in with these, and not be a judge of them.

There are several things that I've been pushing, so to speak, if you haven't noticed: whispering, signing out a napkin. I thought maybe if we got used to these, and sort of accepted them as a community, then in time we could go to our customary and see what we're going to do with it. Now, somebody can say, "Oh, that's his particular target, or that's his particular pet peeve." And that's fine. I don't mind that. But shouldn't there be sort of a giving in, so that we're all somehow identified as belonging here, and we're recognized some way as members of this community?

You know, we take a vow—they call it conversion of life—and that means we're interested in changing. And if we're interested in changing, we should be interested in being corrected, and being challenged.

There is an old saying, "A man convinced against his will is a man unconvinced still." So we have to see whether we're willing to try to stop annoying people. And we have to see whether we're willing to try to stop being annoyed so much by people.

I have two quotes from Cardinal Newman, and I think if you listen to them they'll bring to mind, maybe a little more clearly than my rambling, what I'm trying to say. Let's look at his quote that tells us somehow to deal with annoyance and difference of opinion. It's a long quote. It's good.

Newman wrote to William George Ward, who was the editor of the *Dublin Review*, and his most vocal critic in the public forum. He wrote to William George Ward about how Catholics are divided and think differently. Maybe from this example we can get a point. Writing to Mr. Ward, he says:

I do not feel our differences to be such a trouble

as you do; for such differences always have
been, always will be in the Church; and
Christians would have ceased to have spiritual
and intellectual lives if such differences did not
exist. It is part of their militant state. No human
power can hinder it; nor, if attempted, could it
do more than make a solitude and call it peace.
And thus thinking that man cannot hinder it,
however much he try, I have no great anxiety or
trouble. Man cannot and God will not. He
means such differences to be an exercise of charity. Of course I wish as much as possible to
agree with all my friends, but if, in spite of my
utmost efforts, they go beyond me, or come
short of me, I can't help it, and take it easy.

We were all raised differently; we all think differently.
There's the possibility for a great exercise of charity.

The other quote now—and this is what to do with our
own particular approaches that are annoying to others. This
is Newman again. This is a long quote and, when this one
ends, I will:

We are by nature what we are; very sinful and
corrupt, we know; however, we like to be what
we are, and for many reasons it is very unpleas-
ant for us to change. We cannot change ourselves; this too we know full well, or, at least a
very little experience will teach us. God alone
can change us; God alone can give us the
desires, affections, principles, views, and tastes
which a change implies: this too we know; for I
am all along speaking of men who have a sense
of religion. What then is it that we who profess
religion lack? I repeat it, this: a willingness to be
changed, a willingness to suffer (if I may use
such a word), to suffer Almighty God to change

us. We do not like to let go our old selves; and in whole or part, though all is offered to us freely, we cling to our old selves. Though we were promised no trouble at all in the change, though there were no self-denial, no exertion in changing, the case would not be altered. We do not like to be new-made; we are afraid of it; it is throwing us out of all our natural ways, of all that is familiar to us. We feel as if we should not be ourselves any longer, if we do not keep some portion of what we have been hitherto; and much as we profess in general terms to wish to be changed, when it comes to the point, when particular instances of change are presented to us, we shrink from them, and are content to remain unchanged. *(The Testimony of Conscience).*

To live is to annoy. To live is to be annoyed. I wonder if our living can be less annoying, and I wonder if our living can allow us to be annoyed less. And I think there is some kind of an answer in the customs and the traditions of the house where we all profess our vows, based on a Rule that's proved through the centuries. The conversion of heart and conversion of life is that which leads us from the angelic life here to the real, full angelic life.

Are you willing to change? Am I? We'll see. Amen.

—August 26, 1996

8.

FRATERNAL CORRECTION

We know that poverty, chastity and obedience are vows that come later in the history of religious life. And they, of course, then remain with all of us. But our vows, by identity, are conversion of life and stability. The person who is truly seeking God must change...from what the person is to what the person can become. The person truly seeking God changes in the School of the Lord's Service where no one graduates. The changing, the conversion, is unending; and it's all within the context of stability. The tie is to our monastery, to Saint Meinrad, to its interpretation of conversion, and to its work.

Moving from, moving to conversion, necessarily requires correction and direction. Correction is to come from oneself, and it's to come from one's brothers. It's to come from the abbot and his delegates as superiors. The correction that is spoken of in the Rule is something that must be wanted. Dare I say it's something that must be sought out as part and parcel of the life we're in.

Self-correction, self-direction... from where? It can come from the repentance called for at each Mass as it begins. It can come from the particular examen which should enrich us as a daily practice. It can come from the spiritual direction which we may need to engage in. Self-correction, self-direction, can come from professional counseling, or counseling with one's own confreres or friends. It can come from the sacrament of Penance. It can come from the building of the virtue one is working toward. It can come from the vice one's working against. It can come from conquering the predominant fault.

Correction, conversion, direction, can come from our

brothers. It can come from a word; it can come from a gesture. It can come from compelling example; it can come from jest. My grandmother used to say: "Half in joke, full in earnest." Often a point is made—if the hearer is ready. It can come from the words of a concerned friend. So, correction, direction, can come from anybody we live with.

Correction, direction, can come from our abbot, from his delegates. It can come from the abbot's example and from his teaching. It can from his explicitly pointing out a fault, and from his imposing a penance for a particular fault or attitude.

Correction is something that can be done, and should be done, and often isn't done. Why not? It seems reasonable to say that if one isn't interested in advancing to the running stage of "an enlarged heart in the way of God's command," if one isn't interested, then correction from self is surface. If it comes from others, superiors included, it's annoying; and it may even be judged hypocritical, because the corrector has his own vices too. If one doesn't correct self through the means we mentioned, if correction doesn't start at home, inside oneself, then it's not going to be valued or appreciated coming from others.

Correction given to our neighbor—this is for all of us—is often sparse. For some it's even non-existent. We just don't tell each other. Why? Maybe we think that experience tells us it doesn't work. Maybe we don't want to rock the boat. It may be we're not able to sustain the retort. It may be that we think each one is free and at least 21, and should know enough himself about what's right and wrong. It may be that we think you can't teach an old dog new tricks. It may be that we don't want to be disliked. It may be that we don't in any way view it as our duty. It may be we would rather put up with the fault than risk the results of the correction. It may be we're not emotionally strong enough to say something to someone else.

These excuses can be the same for the abbot, the prior, the subprior, the rector, the provosts, the choirmaster, the master of ceremonies—but the obligation is heavier for these people, and it's heaviest for the abbot. His judgment depends on the exercise of correction, pointing out the right way, noting the wrong.

By these words, I am not encouraging a vigilante approach, for myself or for anyone else, toward anyone. Rather, I'm appealing to all of us to move first of all to a serious concern for self-correction and direction. Is such really needed? I'm convinced it is. I'm convinced it's always needed.

Let's consider some questions we may ask ourselves to get the process I'm proposing off to a start. (I remember giving the retreat in New York to Mother Teresa's Sisters and to Mother Teresa. She asked me if I would do some kind of an examination of conscience for the Sisters, that they could put in their new prayer book. And I did. I thought of that only now.) But some of the questions I want to ask—and I want you to be asking them vicariously—and see what you answer—and be honest—and see if you're willing to do something about the questions.

Do I keep money without permission? Do I purchase or ask for whatever I want and not just what I need? Do I expect others to carry the burden of the *Opus Dei* and the Mass, with my coming as I choose? Is my choice based on what's convenient for me, or how I feel? Do I come back to the monastery to visit betimes? Or do I consider funerals and professions and jubilees times of get-together, gatherings, meant only for those at home? Do I resent being told by the choirmaster that I'm too fast, or I'm too slow, or I'm too loud, or I'm forever coming in too soon? How do I make the choirmaster feel? Is it that some can't be corrected, because it just doesn't work, and there's pouting and there's criticism? I mean, aren't we all supposed to change?

I remember when I had a short term as pro-prior that something came my way—and I had heard this many times before—in reference to a particular monk who went out on the weekends and who preached too long. He was told over and over and over again. And there's a whole stack, I imagine—I haven't looked at anybody's files—of letters saying, "Don't send him here." Couldn't he possibly think, "I preach too long," if everybody says it?

Do I judge some of the house prescriptions juvenile? Am I always the accurate judge and the interpreter of house rules for my personal compliance or rejection? Do I catch on that being hard of hearing isn't a legitimate excuse for me to talk out loud wherever I wish, and to unconsciously set my own pace in choir and at table prayer? Do I care about other people's views on smoking, no matter which side I'm on? Do I ever volunteer for extras, or do I leave that for those I call zealots? Am I annoyed by the differing rubrics and wording of some celebrants, while I don't notice my own peculiarities?: "Oh, he bows. He doesn't genuflect." And I say out loud prayers that shouldn't be. But I don't know that about me; I only know that about him.

Am I an impolite Pharisee in dealing with my brethren, because the fault he has is the only one? Do I at least say hello to all my confreres? When I come into choir do I choose not to go next to that one?

Some of you remember Fr. Blaise. Fr. Blaise wrote *Prayer Starters* for the Abbey Press. Little thoughts. I would like to dub the questions [I posed above] as "self-examination starters." *Ecclesia semper reformanda*—the Church must always be reformed. We're a church. We're the local church here in the monastery. And each one of us is somehow Church. And reformation for us, beyond the ordinary, is somehow a vow. Where stability ties us to one another for the sake of mutually leading each other to God, we do best by letting our light shine, by converting.

If self-correction and direction is tied to the opening moments of Mass, to a particular examen, where we look at ourselves, to counseling, to spiritual direction, to the sacrament of Penance, to the building up of virtue, to the conquering of vice, to the regular opposing of our predominant fault, then we know where to look for help.

But we can say this always, and it brings us to the conclusion: The choice is always ours. Nobody can make us do it. Will we choose to listen to what we've heard tonight? Please God we will. We have all kinds of problems; we always will. But we have one way of life and it calls for constant change.

(It's funny. I think of somebody who is forever saying that everybody is too slow. Could it have ever entered his mind that he's too fast?)

We have lots to tell each other. We have lots to show each other. And we have a lot to do on our own. You know that quote from St. Augustine: "Pray as if all depends on God, and work as if all depends on self." Let's move ahead, and keep moving ahead, and keep moving ahead, and they'll know there's something special about that monastery in southern Indiana. Amen.

—October 14, 1996

9.

A Period Of Reclaiming

My dear brothers...

L ent is to be a reclaiming time. It's to be a time when we put our hat on straight again. St. Benedict says that Lent is a time to live as we should always be living. We need to ask why is such a time as Lent needed, and then to ask why is it needed every year, and then to ask why is it needed now.

It's needed because we've all got fallen—or maybe more accurately—ever-falling human nature. Our wounded nature requires Lent. Such a time as Lent is an absolute must for a sinner, a sinner who is seeking God.

Cardinal Newman says, "Let us define ourselves for what we really are: sinners, at most, attempting to do good." Cardinal Newman says, "We are people who learn to do right from having done wrong." Cardinal Newman says, "Our nature is such that we go into heaven backwards."

Lent is meant to be a wrong-to-right period, a time to turn things around once more, a time to move once again toward the right direction, the direction...

stage for all the world to wonder about.

We came here to seek God, and we have no other reason for remaining here in this holy place, where God-seeking is reason for its existence. Seeking God is Benedictine. Here, in this holy place, is Saint Meinrad, Saint Meinrad, Indiana. Our course of action must always be based on a specific vow. It's called conversion of life. We all pronounced it, without exception. We're all held to it without exception. There is no shaking it off, so long as we're Benedictines. 1997 is the present year of salvation. It's the "today" in which we are to hear his voice. It's all we have; it's our now. The hope and the helps for this desired change are the grace of the season and the openness of our hearts to its power.

To make our presentation simple (and St. Alphonsus Ligouri says, "I always, no matter to whom I preach, preach so that the most illiterate laborer can understand me.") —to make our presentation simple, we say, "We either seek God or we seek self. We either seek God or we seek self, for seek we must."

- If we keep back money, or spend money, and money is not ours, whether we live within the monastery or outside the monastery as our assignment places us, we seek self.
- If we base choir attendance on convenience or how we feel, we seek self.
- If we don't fulfill the obligation to pray the Divine Office, we seek self.
- If we work for the community and don't associate with the community, we seek self.
- If we must have the latest book and the clothes and the shoes of the hour, we seek self.
- If running out to meals and associating with outside friends is seemingly all-important, we seek self.
- If we are upset when things don't go our way, and we fashion our way as the way, we seek self.
- If we identify ourselves as "a morning person," or

"an evening person," and then we keep our own personal schedule, we seek self.

- If we're filled with personal principles—"It's a principle of mine," we say—and thereby refuse to give in, we doubly seek self.

The ifs of self-seeking can go on endlessly. We can all supply many more examples of them, and, of course, we take the examples from people other than ourselves. Yet, on a clear day, there's a blessed possibility of our seeing where we ourselves seek self. And Lent is meant to be that clear day.

Now, I know that St. Benedict warns the abbot against driving the flock too much on one day, even if it's a clear day, and even if it's Lent. And I know that St. Benedict warns the abbot against breaking the vessel from too much rubbing. And yet I say, nonetheless, quoting Angela Merici, that "self will (self-seeking) is a veritable hell's fire." We must face that truth, like it or not.

St. Benedict says, *"Sunt viae quae videntur ab hominibus rectae, quorum fines usque ad profundum inferni demergit."*— "There are ways which seem to men to be correct, whose ends take one to the pit of hell."

And so I must ask, as Lent begins, without too much driving or without too much rubbing, can we not individually work seriously on at least one expression of self-will that takes us from seeking God and keeps us wallowing in self-

Easter this year can be better than ever. Pray God it will be. The choice is ours. The choice is always ours, for the grace of God is never lacking, and the grace of God and choice are the only two components necessary. If we choose the grace of the season, then we can say with St. Paul, as St. Benedict quotes him in the Prologue, because we have chosen *"gratia Dei sum quod sum"*—"I am what I am by the grace of God." If we can say this truthfully, then we can say we're seeking God. And if we can say we're seeking God, then we can say we're Benedictine. And we can say the monastery of Saint Meinrad is a place of holiness. And we can say, without saying it, without shining our light but merely letting our light shine, we can say, "Come here. We'll show you the way."

There is no lesson needed in this world more than that: to show people the way. This is our calling; this is what we pledge. The moment is at hand. Let us screw up our courage, and let us move forward. Because today his voice calls, and the only thing that will hold us back is a hard heart.

My brothers, it's a glorious season. It's the season when we can change. All we have to do is listen to God instead of listening to self. St. Thérèse says, "Let the good God choose for me. It's what he wants that I love." Pope John Paul II said at his jubilee—and how wonderful it would be if we could all say this—"I have let the Lord lead me along the ways he set before me. I've done it day after day." Amen.

—*Feb. 12, 1997*